# DEVELOPMENT AND CHANGE

**About the Editor**

The editor of the book Professor S.P. Nagendra is a distinguished sociologist currently holding the position of Director at the Govind Ballabh Pant Social Science Institute, Allahabad. He is the author of several learned papers including his book on 'The Concept of Ritual in Modern Sociological Theory'.

# DEVELOPMENT AND CHANGE

## Emerging Perspectives

*Edited by*
S.P. NAGENDRA
*Director*
Govind Ballabh Pant Social Science Institute
Allahabad

CONCEPT PUBLISHING COMPANY, NEW DELHI 110059

ISBN 81-7022-526-4

First Published 1994



*Published and Printed by*
Ashok Kumar Mittal
Concept Publishing Company
A/15-16, Commercial Block, Mohan Garden
NEW DELHI 110059 (India)

*Lasertypeset by*
Printing Express
H-13, *Bali Nagar*
NEW DELHI 110015

# PREFACE

The papers collected in this volume are a token of our participation in the ongoing debate on development and social change. Pretty old though, the debate can never lose its edge nor can it ever lose its relevance, which makes its fitting that we keep it going. Written for different occasions and from different angles, the papers nevertheless hang together well, reflecting the common conviction of the authors that development is no mere maximisation of economic welfare conceived either in terms of a rising standard of living or as an ever improving quality of life; but essentially a process of creative change in which man constantly discovers and rediscovers himself to become, what he has in him to become, without any external aid or assistance, not excluding organised religion either.

Changes in the economy, society and ecology are an integral part of development. For it is through these changes that man tries to create an environment which appeals to him and which augments his *being*. Any change in the environment beyond this point becomes ugly, over-exploitative and counter-productive. Change for development, in other words, is a normative process, which in no case can be reduced to a value-neutral exercise. Therefore, if the increasing imbalance in the three layers of the environment is to be corrected and their symbiosis to be restored, then a genuine search has to begin for values, which will not only provide the true normative setting to development but also act as its driving force Nor can this shift in values be brought about by a paper revolution in values – by coining, that is to say, innovative catchwords like "Think globally – act locally", "Small is beautiful" and so on. What is really called for is a replacement of the values of the existing unidimensional society, viz., the values of acquisition and expansion, of egotism and competition, by those of inner growth and conservation; of altruism and cooperation. Inner growth, conservation, cooperation, and altruism are not utopian values. On the other hand, they occupy the pride of place in all traditions. However, it is not their revival that is contemplated – in fact, their revival is just not possible. What is contemplated however is the discovery of fresh meanings behind them, consistent with the urges and aspirations of mankind today.

If this little book could stimulate fresh thinking on the subject, I and my colleagues would deem our labours rewarded.

I must acknowledge the help I have received from my colleagues in organising this publication. While I am grateful to them all for their cooperation, my thanks are due particularly to Professor L.R. Singh on whose time I have always had an unrestricted claim, and who this time too has been as generous to me as ever. My most sincere thanks to Dr. Suresh Mishra but for whose keen interest in the project, the book could not have gone to the press. Last but not least I must thank Sri Anjesh Kumar and Sri Ratan Lal for doing a neat job of typing the manuscript.

S.P. NAGENDRA

# CONTENTS

## LIST OF TABLES



## LIST OF FIGURES

# LIST OF CONTRIBUTORS

**Anjesh Kumar**, Computer Programmer

**Bhatt, K.N.,** Research Assistant in Economics

**Bimal Kumar,** Research Associate in Economics

**Giri, Ananta,** Research Associate in Anthropology

**Mishra, Suresh,** Research Assistant in Political Science

**Nagendra, S.P.**, Director

**Pant, S.K.**, Research Associate in Economics

**Sharma, A.D.,** Senior Fellow in Economics

**Singh, L.R.,** Professor of Geography

**Srivastava, K.B.**, Senior Fellow in Political Science

**Tewari, G.C.**, Reader in Economics

**Tripathi, Raj Mani**, Research Assistant in Geography

**ONE**

# THE THEORY OF DEVELOPMENT : A Sociological Critique

S.P. NAGENDRA

Even most serious questions sometime get bogged down in tendentious debates because they are vitiated by the very manner of their formulation. The question of development or the wider question of social change is one such question which was formulated with presupposed answers with the result that the concepts and theories which have grown about it over the years, have not only tended to deflect it from the central issues involved in it, but imparted to it an ideological slant.

The misformulation of the question in sociology is bound up with the misformulation of the sociological problem itself. The problem before the founding fathers of sociology, as they could see it, was not what the social reality was, but how it was to be brought under the coverage of the scientific method. Their preoccupation, in other words, was not with the nature of social reality, but with the scientific method, whose infallibility as a source of valid knowledge had to be established with reference to the social reality also, a preoccupation which eventually led to the reduction of the ontic to the epistemic. The method had already yielded a concept of nature as determined by the laws of space, time and causalty, laws about whose universality, all doubts had been set at rest by Kant. But the social reality consisted of minded and free beings, an intuition whose validity the sociologists never questioned. The feat, then, of bringing it under the paramountcy of the scientific laws could not be achieved unless the realm of freedom was equated with the realm of unfreedom. The equation was crucial as the very possibility of sociology as a science rested on it. The sociologists then had no option but to demonstrate by hook or by crook that the social reality was nothing but a variety of the natural or in other words, it was what the scientific method would make of it. They did this; and by a tricky misformulation of the basic question before them. Instead of asking what kind of reality is the social reality, they asked : what kind of natural reality is the social reality? And the obvious answer was : it is a para-natural reality. It is this 'category mistake'[1] on which sociology started building its theories; and the science has matured in the same proportion as it has succeeded in reducing the social to the natural. It is neither necessary nor possible to show how the aim of the entire range of sociological thinking from Comte to Parsons via Marx, it has been to highlight the nature-image of human society. In other words, to view it as a self-regulating, self-perpetuating and self-transforming reality which commands, constraints, and socialises the individual and which is no less at peace and harmony with itself than nature. The gap between what it is and what it tends to be is no doubt always there in society. But it is constantly at pains to fill this gap; it has its own in-built mechanisms which perpetually resolve its internal tensions and tend to keep it in a state of equilibrium.

We may now see how the theory of development derives from this official theory of society. But in the meanwhile we must consider an objection which may be pertinently raised against our thesis. Is it possible, it may be asked, for sociology to escape this reductionist predicament? To say that the nature of reality should determine the method of its study, is to say nothing, as there is no way to ascertain the nature of reality without reference to the method of its study. In fact there is no escape from the position that the ontic is relative to the epistemic unless the two are viewed as parts of a hierarchy participating in a nondual metaphysic which transcends them both. Social science methodology then must be firmly grounded in metaphysics if it is to be saved from its inherent solipsism and if it is to ensure an adequate understanding of social reality. Even the methodologies of structural anthropology and phenomenological sociology fall short of this requirement, despite their unquestionable superiority over other methodologies.

It should be clear from what has been said about the nature of sociological theory that it must consider development as a change from a lower state of social order to a higher state, it being assumed that the model of the higher state is the harmony present in nature. Whether it is conceived as increasing 'positive mentality' as in Comte, or as increasing 'differentiation and coherence', as in Spencer, or as increasing 'rationality' as in Pareto, Weber and Durkheim[2] or as 'enhancement of adaptive capacity' as in Parsons, or as increasing 'communicative rationality' as in Herbermas, it is in any case a change from a lower non-human state to a higher non-human state. Nor is there much to distinguish on this score between these theories and that of Karl Marx either. Development for Karl Marx also means increasing social quality and increasing self-regulativeness of human society. Even the state as an institution of regulation and control par excellence has no place in Marx's utopia.

It is interesting to note that the sociological concept of rationality means nothing but adaptability to nature when it comes to man-nature opposition, and social conformity when it comes to individual-society opposition. "Freedom" said Hegel is "the recognition of necessity", words which were echoed by Marx also. But what eventually becomes of freedom, thanks to the line of development sociology has taken, is the ability to act in conformity with social necessity. To be free is to act rationally, and to act rationally is to act in conformity with social necessity. The protest against what has come to be known as the concept of 'oversocialised' man in contemporary sociology is a protest against the concept of socially overconstrained man. It is again, against this concept of man that comes the voice of protest from philosophers like Sartre and Heidegger. We will return to the problem of human freedom at a later stage in our discussion.

Thus understood development becomes synonymous with linear change implying a point of beginning and a point of end, of which the former is the lower point and the latter the higher. But a theory of linear change can be maintained only at the cost of rejecting the logic of change. For how can we talk of change without reference to that which changes. If change, as Kant put it, were to consist in the possibility of 'a conjunction of contradictorily opposed predicates in one and the same object',[3] then change cannot be intuited without its dialectical opposite viz, permanence. But permanence in the like manner, cannot be thought of without change; for how can we talk of that which changes without reference to the possibility of its becoming otherwise.

There has been much debate in philosophy on whether permanence is real and change illusion, or change a reality and permanence an appearance; the first position being attributed to philosophers like Zeno and Samkara and the second to those like Heraclitus and Nagarjuna.[4] But this again is a false attribution to both the groups of philosophers none of whom makes any mistake about the complementarity of permanence and change, of being and becoming, of the primordial and the temporal.[5] As part of a dialectical pair of opposites change has the potentiality of becoming permanence and permanence the possibility of becoming contingent. From permanence to change and from change to permanence is a cyclic movement. "Everything that is, everything substantive and living has its normal mode of growth declared Heraclitus and so ex hypothesi does it have its cycle. For all living things manifestly undergo cycles of genesis and decay, of life and death".[6] As Heraclitus, so also did Plato and Aristotle recognise the cyclicality of change. For Plato, 'eternity is but an endless succession' of cycles. "Invariably one of these cycles is held to terminate in some great catastrophe, usually a flood .... with but a handful of individuals left alive to commence the next cycle of civilization.[7] And for Aristotle also 'the coming to be of anything, if it is absolutely necessary, that is, moving in the way it is so constituted to move "must be cyclical".[8] The central point in the whole classical Greek philosophy of change as Nisbet[9] points out is the concept of 'physis'. Everything whether it was a tree, dog, man himself or the cosmos, was supposed to have its physis, its disposition to grow. Aristotle's words, in the statement cited above, — 'moving in the way it is so constituted to move-' mean nothing more nor less than what the idea of physis implies. Heraclitus compared physis to a 'moral police' meaning thereby that if things do not grow the way they should grow, that is, according to their 'physis', retribution will be swift'.

There is a remarkable similarity between the Greek idea of 'physis' and the Indian idea of *swabhava*, the nature, the intrinsic attribute of a thing which makes it what it is and prevents it from being anything else. *Swabhava* is a manifestation of the primordial *being* in the contingent *becoming* and so is 'physis'.

Thus in traditional thought, both Greek and Indian, development means becoming according to the law of one's nature, 'a determinable sequence of changes proceeding from the very structure of a thing' as Aristotle put it. The dialectical opposite of development is decay, that is, change whose sequence cannot be determined, which is, that is to say, unnatural or accidental. The possibility of decay is contained in development as the possibility of development is contained in decay. However, decay is not the same thing as cosmic catastrophe of Plato's conception. The latter signifies the end of Time itself when becoming is reabsorbed into Being, the end of one day of the cosmic creator, Brahma in the Indian tradition.[10] Significantly the end of Time is equated with the reduction of everything to the Waters, in the Indian tradition also. The residues in Plato's case are 'a few shepherds high in the hills' and in the Indian case the cosmic Serpent called the residue or the *Shesha* and the archetypal Man reclining on it in the cosmic Waters.

Decay and development are processes within time and hence the interregnum between the two can be filled only by an atemporal agency which may stop the drift and initiate development afresh. One may call it a charismatic personality in the language of sociology or a divine incarnation in the terminology of the living religions.

If we keep this plain logic of social change in mind, we cannot entertain the linear theory of self-realising and self-fulfilling change with the primitive society as its starting point and the contemporary western society as its end. Not that the protagonists of the theory are unaware of its loopholes; they do realise that change cannot be thought of without persistence. Not do they rule out the possibility of deviant or anomic tendencies developing within the social organisation. But they consider them all *sub specie tempori.* Persistence is as much an attribute of time for them, as is change, and so are also order and anomie. In fact the social reality for them is both Being and becoming.

Even the structural theory of social change in the existentialist phenomenological formulation, is not free from this mistake. Edward A. Tiryakian, for instance, talks both of structuration and destructuration of social reality, equivalents roughly of development and decay. He even admits that the 'ground of any genuine social revolution is an attempted overturning and radical rotation of the normative axis which frames and orders institutional life'. Again societal change in his view 'stems from those who are religious radicals alien to or alienated from the normative order of the ongoing society'. Tiryakian is equally clear in his mind that the genesis of social change cannot be located in the political or even the economic order. But social reality for him, too, is a temporal reality containing in itself both Being and becoming : the existential ground of possibilities — the social structure as well as the actualisation of this ground into social institutions.[11]

This is the ridiculous situation in which modern theory of social change places itself. But be it as it may, the theory received a big boost from intellectuals in the west because it not only established, once for all, the superiority of western society over all others, but also justified its paternalistic—imperialistic attitude towards them. The comparative method had shown the contrast between development as exemplified in the European society and stagnation as exemplified in what now came to be called 'primitive' and 'intermediate societies'.[12]

## II

It was in the context of these societies that the question of development was raised and particularly after the Second World War when many of them emerged into history after a long spell of colonial rule. Within the official theory of development there was only one answer to the question, and it was that if these societies wanted to transform their sub-human existence, they must follow the example of their European counterparts. In other words, they must imitate the European model of development, which meant adopting all that Europe, including its alter ego America, stood for, in one word, modernity; and rejecting all that these societies themselves represented, in one word, tradition. Since the western world itself had, in the due course of time, become split into two worlds, modernity also got bifurcated into two models, which for convenience's sake we may describe as right-wing modernity and left-wing modernity. Thus within the basic dichotomy of the metropolitan and dependent worlds, the global society gets further differentiated into right-wing metropolis, left-wing metropolis and the dependencies.[13] The dependencies could either adopt the modernity of the right wing or the modernity of the left wing or partly both the two, if they so chose, in which case, they would enjoy the patronage of both the worlds.

The distinction that we have made between the three subdivisions of the global society, is of a piece with the distinction made between the First World, the Second World and the Third World, in the language of international relations.[14] The relationship between the First and Second Worlds is one of opposition, but in their unity they constitute a solid block of opposition to the Third World. It is this kind of opposition, this kind of relationship of dominence and dependence, which characterises the drama of international relations within the contemporary global society. The drama gets going through massive economic aid from the metropolis to the Third World in the name of sympathy and help, and through an unbroken indoctrination of the intellectuals in the Third World by their mentors in the metropolis. Within the global society it is the intellectuals who constitute the link between the metropolis and the dependencies and within the dependencies, between the ruling elites and the people. The intellectuals in the Third World silently receive the message from the First and Second Worlds and propogate it to their people who can neither understand nor reciprocate it.

Thanks to the setting of the global drama, the developing world also gets artificially split into two worlds : one that of the dominant elites and the other that of the dependent people. The elites are obviously the agents of modernisation or development and the people, virtually its patients. They are patients because their lot is only to suffer; for what they are preached to do has hardly anything to do with their development; its sole purpose being to keep the show of development going, may be to lull them into silence. Incidentally, both in relation to the people and the dominant elites, the intellectuals, right-wingers and left-wingers alike, find themselves sailing in the same boat. Both are equally alienated from the people and equally aligned with the ruling elites. Nor is it by sheer accident that there is such a big gap between the intellectuals and the people, and little or no gap between the intellectuals and the ruling elites. What Julien Benda[15] calls the betrayal of intellectuals is only a logical outcome of the value premises implicit in modernity.

But even if we grant that adoption of modernity is the essence of development, the question would still arise whether or not this adoption necessarily implies a rejection of tradition. No, it does not; is one answer to the question, but the official answer and hence, worthy of serious consideration. If caste is influencing politics in modern India, if that is to say, it has become a parapolitical community, the only reason could be that it had the potentiality to become so, for how else could a traditional institution like caste become a modern political institution like a pressure group. Where then is the incompatibility between tradition and modernity? Tradition is simply underdeveloped modernity and modernity, developed tradition. This is how the Rudolphs argue.[16] Again if Indians could continue becoming more modern every day without ceasing to be Indian any bit, how could there be an opposition between tradition and modernity? "In India" writes Milton Singer[17] "modernisation takes the form of traditionalisation". There is no substantial difference between the stands taken by the Rudolphs and Milton Singer on this score; both arrive at the same conclusion and by the same method of fallacious reasoning. Their conclusion is that tradition is no bar to India's modernisation; and their argument is that even though apparently different from modernity, tradition is basically convertible into modernity. As though there was nothing new in change (modernity) and the future was a sheer unfoldment of the past (tradition).

Almost the same is the upshot of M.N. Sriniva's[18] well known theory of sanskritisation and westernisation. The theory explains ongoing change in Indian society as an upward mobility of the lower, non-elite castes through adoption of the cultural values of the Brahman elites and a similar vertical mobility of the Brahman elites through adoption of the cultural values of their western rulers, almost a case of the little tradition transforming itself into the great tradition and the great tradition changing itself into modernity.

Almost all western and Indian social scientists who have participated in the debate on social change, by and large, voice the same opinion, each of course, in his own way.[19] In fact there is little to distinguish even between the right wingers and left wingers as regards their commitment to the official theory. Both have their affiliation with the metropolis and both orchestrate the opinion relayed to them from their respective camps.

The specious piece of theorising which gives rise to the theory of modernity of tradition, also gives a new slant to the theory of development. For once it is admitted that tradition can take modernity in its stride, the difference between the underdeveloped traditional and the developed modern societies, becomes just a matter of time lag and by the same logic development becomes a matter of speeding up the ongoing change. The theory of development in the context of these societies, then, takes the form of a theory of guided change, and the theory of guided change in turn becomes a theory of techno-economic change. Because, when it comes to the question of closing time lag, technology is the best answer. Thus on the sociologist's own showing, the theory of development in underdeveloped societies is nothing but a theory of planned techno-economic change.

Now, if it is the economist who holds the key to the development of the Third World, then an Adam Smith of poverty, like Gunnar Myrdal is the only hope for the underdogs of this World. But even Gunnar Myrdal[20] or the economists whose theories he rejects to establish the vanguard status of his own theory, have their own difficulties in making the social reality responsive to their formula. Tradition, which in the economists' manner of theorising now becomes a symbol for the whole array of non-economic values, cannot just be reduced to para-modern, or para-economic values and managed like economic values. What then happens is that when an institutional theory of development like the one proposed by Myrdal also fails to click with the reality, the failure of the theory is blamed upon the 'softness' of the underdeveloped people themselves. Economists[21] like Myrdal are theoretically determined to believe that lethargy, indiscipline, corruption, and social injustice, are part and parcel of the very life-style of the underdeveloped world. Likewise when measures of land reform fail to deliver the goods in India, the Planning Commission's Task Force on Agrarian Relations must blame the ruling elites for their failure to implement these measures with a strong political will and the political wing of the ruling elites must blame its bureaucratic counterpart or else the opposition parties or the people themselves, for their lack of co-operation with the government.

The prevailing anomie in India's public life is not a result of her slow pace of adaptation to the modernising ideals. It is, on the other hand, an outcome of her stubborn resistance to these ideals, her refusal to accept and legitimise them. For the adoption of these ideals would mean a complete overturning of her normative axis for which India does not yet seem ready. But that does not mean that she cannot overcome her artificial crisis of poverty and backwardness which she has inherited from history. In their overzealous concern for India's poverty let economists and social scientists not forget that long before her encounter with the modernising ideals, India had achieved a measure of economic prosperity which was the envy of the West. Aurobindo[22] writes "the splendour of Asiatic and not least of Indian prosperity, the wealth of Ormuz and of Ind, the barbaric doors rough with gold .... were once stigmatised by the less opulent west as a sign of barbarism. Circumstances are now strangely reversed; the opulent barbarism and much less artistic ostentation of wealth are to be found in London, New York and Paris, and it is the nakedness of India and the squalor of her poverty which are flung in her face as evidence of the worthlessness of her culture".

A traditional society's resistance to the modernising ideals is as natural as the resistance of the sacred to the profane. In a traditional society where man is viewed *sub specie aeternitatis*—as a becoming of Being the social institutions are regarded as exemplifications of the primordial Law. But just the reverse is the case with modern society, where man is considered *sub specie tempori*, — as a creature of history — and the social institutions as sedimentations of group habits sanctified by reason. Where reason is the supreme principle of validation of values and norms, science and technology must become the governing principles of life, as they are the foremost instruments of reason. Again, when science and technology become the governing principles of life, the norms and values created by them become the norms and values of life itself. Myths, mysteries and the ultimate values, in terms of which all problematic situations in life are traditionally explained are expelled from life and their place is taken by science and technology.

This is the stage which society in the West has reached in the course of its development, a stage at which life stands completely demythologised, and technology glorified into a new but superior myth of life. The net result is a dehumanisation of life, a substitution of life by a system of fake human values and artificial institutional means of realising them. It is therefore not without reason that there is a loud and articulate cry[23] in the West itself against the fake and pretentious Messiah[24], 'the enemy of intellect[25] that is science and the 'one dimensional society[26] that is the modern industrial civilisation. The predicament of the western intellectual, however, is that when he feels oppressed by the institutions he has himself created he turns into a critical humanist or becomes an existentialist or postmodernist and cries for freedom; only that he cannot step out of the unfreedom in which he finds himself strait-jacketed. But the man in Asia, howsoever, unfortunate otherwise, is fortunate at least in one respect that he still has a chance to retrieve his freedom and to save himself from the unfreedom of the fortunate man in the West.

How he can do so, is a question into which for obvious reasons we cannot enter here. But let us make no mistake about the fact that it is futile to think of freedom and development within the framework of the official theory, following which India has already done enough damage to her economy, polity and society.

Having been brainwashed for over a century and a half to believe that we had so far belonged to a bad society which we must now discard, we started destroying one by one all our traditional institutions, almost with a vengeance, soon after becoming independent. And alongside of this process of detraditionalisation, went also modernisation : legitimisation of the colonial institutions and autocolonisation of our own institutions. In the result what we have been able to achieve so far, in lieu of a good society is a set of elitist social institutions not only alien to our tradition but wholly out of tune with the urges and aspirations of the people. Take any sublayer, or the overlayer of modernity now covering the traditional base of the Indian society and you will see the gap between the common man — the real man — and the artificial social institutions he has to contend with. Place him in the context of any of these institutions and you will see that he is more a victim thereof than a beneficiary.

Take our system of centralist planning in which the needs of the common man are determined by an elitist agency. The only role that the common man is expected to play in this system of planning is to follow the directions of the experts. There are numerous studies showing that the benefits of planning are not reaching the common man. There is a growing realisation among the experts themselves that development has failed to ensure social justice. Is not then the common man a mere object, a victim, of planning? Those who harboured the hope that contradictions in our theory of planning could be corrected by giving it a socialist twist are as much disillusioned as the protagonists of the conventional theory. In a theory where development means an artificial expansion of needs and a continued search for provisions to meet these needs, it is impossible to ensure social justice except in an arbitrary manner.

Let me illustrate. If development means a rising standard of living, it implies an ever improving consumption basket, which in turn would mean rising wages, rising costs of production and rising prices. Therefore, even if birth rate could be controlled and full employment ensured, wages cannot be equalised and a gap must always remain between the poor whose wages cannot permit them to go for better consumption baskets and the affluent, who will press the economic system to produce newer and better consumption baskets for them. Even the developed societies are finding it difficult to control prices and to contain the poverty inherent in the logic of affluent development.

In an elitist theory of planning, industry is bound to get priority over agriculture and the city over the village. From the way we talk of rural development, is not the impression created that the rural society is an unnecessary appendage to the urban society? We may or not admit this fact but our whole attitude to the villages is one of commiseration mixed with contempt, almost the same kind of attitude that the metropolitan World has towards the Third World. If the villages want to develop, they must adopt the urban way of life and since they can not do so on their own, the cities must help them. But it is not without reservation that the urban elites talk of the development of the villages. There is a push-pull theory of urbanisation which tells us in so many words that the villages are congenitally poor and overbreeding and a constant source of overcrowding to the cities. Therefore, while planning for rural development we must also plan for the defence of the cities against the invasion of the villages.

To say, that modernisation is a false goal of development is one thing, but to say that it is luxury, India in her present circumstances cannot afford is, another. The cities must get priority over the villages in all matters pertaining to development because if the cities are the models which the villages must imitate, they must be made truly worthy of imitation.

In the circumstances, all that we can think of doing for the villages, in the name of development is symbolic modernisation which is already under way. It is another thing that the reaction of the villages even to a limited dose of modernisation should be so wild. If village life is chaotic today as never before, and there is now greater exploitation of the villagers by political vested-interests than heretofore, the reason is not that the theory is defective, but as the ruling elite would have us believe, the people are backward and superstitious!

Space would not permit us to enter into a detailed discussion of the relationship between villages and cities in a traditional society. Suffice it to say that they are structural segments of one and the same cultural whole and are bound by a relationship of complementarity rather than fundamental opposition. The development of one at the cost of the other would therefore, mean a violation of the very structural law of the development of the whole. As parts of the whole, they have to develop complementing each other's development and promoting in turn the life of the whole. Contemporary urban sociology starts which rural-urban dichotomy and ends with rural-urban continuum a euphemism for the concept of the village as a subsidary of the city. Urbanisation which is basically the same thing as growth of class inequalities[27], a characteristic of industrial urban societies is shown to be the natural tendency of rural change. It is such theories of ongoing rural change that provide the feedback to the official theory of development, in which the village practically becomes a casuality.

## III

We can see how the modern history of development which begins as an answer to a false question ultimately degenerates into an ideology and becomes a vested interest in the hands of its protagonists. And it is this sinister implication of the theory, its inherent tendency to become an ideology of manipulation and control which the so-called underdeveloped societies have to guard against. In fact if they want to survive and develop as free nations, they have to free their freedom from the octopus-hold of the institutions, which have stemmed from the theory, institutions which both in their design and action are meant to control them.

An alternative[28] theory of development for India and for the Third World must then begin with what Paulo Freire[29] calls 'cultural action for freedom'. This will mean in the first place, a new education of the people to break the culture of science, in which they have been brought up so far. Once this culture is broken and the people begin to speak, they will themselves realise the threat the elitist institutions pose to their existence and freedom. In the second place, cultural action for freedom will mean the creation of an institutional set-up suited to the people's own genius, which is the *sine qua non* of free development. What the task presupposes is not a paper revolution in values, but a radical change in outlook which can be brought about only by a cultural renaissance. Let us not labour under the illusion that the foundation of a healthy national life can be laid on the modernising ideals. We have to rediscover our identity in the traditions of our indigeneous culture and then refashion our national institutions in accordance with its own living ideals. The search of this identity had begun during our national struggle for independence with the Swadeshi movement launched by Gandhi, when a cultural renaissance seemed to be in the offing. The Shanti Niketan, Kashi Vidyapith, Bihar Vidyapith, the Banaras Hindu University, the Jamia Millia to mention only the institutions of higher learning, were flowers of a resurgent national culture, whose principal aim it was to lay the foundation of a national pattern of higher education suited to our culture. None had a greater realisation of the futility of the colonial system of education, than Tagore, Malviya and Gandhi. Even these institutions have lost their identity and now form part of the same sterile system of national education that we have evolved after independence, a system whose worthlessness cannot be judged only by its total rejection by the younger generations whose increasing anger and growing sense of indiscipline is no part of their cultural inheritance.

But the renaissance which began during the national movement came to a sudden halt soon after independence when the creative elites became power-elites and their creativity gave way to 'mechanical mimesis' to use a Toynbee phrase. And thus began the authentication of colonial legacies and the imitation of modernising ideals in the name of development. And the result is there for all of us to see. India's cultural pluralism is nothing new, only the deep fissions in her body social manifesting in endemic communal and caste conflicts are a recent phenomenon. A nation opposed to its own language is at odds with its own spirit. But thanks to elitist vested interests this is what the situation has come to be in India.

Unity within a culturally pluralist society cannot be thought of except within the framework of primordial human values which constitute the core of all cultural traditions and yet transcend them each individually. Primordial values never die except metaphorically when their meanings are forgotten or when they get reduced to superstitions. A rediscovery of their meanings, is a discovery of new and fresh potentialities in the human spirit. This is what we mean by cultural renaissance — a creative change from stagnation to development which is to be distinguished both from cultural reform and cultural revival. Revival of exhausted possibilities is impossible and reform often takes the form of imposition of group ideology on living social laws. It is the creative elites who are the agents par excellence of renaissant change.

The distinction is necessary because an archaist ideology has also become a contender of the modernist ideology as an alternative philosophy of development in India. Indianisation[30] as advocated by a section of Indian intellectuals has both a revivalist and reformist tinge. Perpetuating it in its outworn form and imposing it on other cultural traditions is a wrong answer to the question of cultural pluralism; it is yet another method of manipulative control which, as we have shown, is the implicit assumption of the modernist ideology.

There is no fundamental opposition between the cultural traditions of the so-called majority and minority communities of India; they are contingent modalities of the same set of primordial values. It is for the creative elites to demonstrate in communicable words and imitable images that the diverse cultural traditions of India are segments of the same whole and that there is no mutual, contradiction between them. There is no conflict either between any of these traditions and the ideals of freedom, justice and equality on which, we avowedly want to build our national life. For no tradition has ever despised freedom; no tradition has ever scorned justice and no tradition has ever been averse to equality before law. They are perennial human values and by no manner of means the Western society's unique gift to humanity.

They come in conflict with tradition only when they are juxtaposed to it in their modern inverted forms. The traditional man has no difficulty in understanding natural justice but he finds it difficult to understand modern justice, mediated, costly and delayed, which often runs counter to his own sense of natural justice. He knows his *dharma* and also knows that it is *dharma* that rules and the king only reigns, but he cannot understand the intricate rule of law in which men rule and the law only reigns. This explains the traditional man's aversion to modern values which he cannot place anywhere in his real life.

Nor is it a case of tradition versus reason, for reason has its own place in the traditional hierarchy of values. It is subordinate to intellect[31] and can never aspire to supersede it except at the cost of its own identity. Reason, that is to say, presupposes a transnational principle of guidance in the absence of which it can exist only as unfettered rationality. And it is this unfettered rationally that is the name of reason constituting the central point in modernity. Therefore, there can be no question of a synthesis of tradition and modernity.[32]

But the compatibility of development with tradition is as axiomatic as its incompatibility with modernity. Development a la modernity is a manipulation of man and society according to a set formula devised by a historically successful group. But development a la tradition is growth of man and society according to the law of their being, according to their 'physis' as the Greek tradition would have it, or according to their *swabhava* as the Indian tradition has it. A theory of development, therefore, presupposes an adequate understanding of tradition and culture whose source is myth and folklore now consigned to the limbo by contemporary sociology.

It would be wrong to believe that India's economic problem is more pressing than the political or that the political is more important than the cultural. It would be equally incorrect to assume that the solution of the economic problem ensures the solution of all other problems. In fact there can be no economic development without political stability and there can be no political stability without a real consensus on the ends of political action. In a democracy based on real consensus there can be no gap between the ruling elites and the people; such a gap can exist only in an opinionated democracy like the one India has borrowed from the West. Traditional polities are based on real consensus — on unanimity — where there is collective ideation and where aristocracy takes the form of democracy. Modern polities, on the other hand, are based on manipulated consensus — a majority opinion — where there is only formal discussion instead of ideation and where democracy takes the form of aristocracy. The only ground from which we can expect the emergence of a unanimous polity, is tradition, the store-house of archetypes and primordial values. And a unanimous polity alone can sustain a cultural unity under which different cultures can grow and flourish without fear of anyone being absorbed into another.[33]

If development means man's becoming what he has in him to become, in other words, his self-realisation, as is the implication of the concept in all traditions, then the ends of development cannot be served by a 'consensual democracy where the individuals' 'communicative competence' is determined by the vested interests of his political party and where the individual himself has been shaped and socialised to serve the needs of the system, rather than the system serving his own needs. It was not without reason then, that Gandhi not only despised modernity in all its forms but rejected the entire paraphernalia of modern civilisation as utterly unsuited to the normal development of humanity. Gandhi's love for *swadeshi*, traditional village communities, a need rather than acquisition-oriented economy organised round the virtues of *asteya*, and *aparigraha* (non-stealing and non-acquisitiveness) can be matched only by his relentless opposition to universalised, abstract and impersonalised systems of education, health and law, etc. which could never serve genuine ends of life.

A full length discussion of Gandhi's social philosophy, particularly his scheme of social reconstruction will not be possible here. But let there be no doubt about the fact that there is no better answer, to date, to the challenge of globalised Fordism[34] with all its sinister implications for the so-called developing societies, than Gandhi. There is, of course, no dearth of scholars and social activists who still believe that modernity could be tamed and yoked with tradition to produce a better world than the one to which we have willy-nilly come to belong.[35]

If taming modernity means putting reason in place, which will be tantamount to divesting it of its autonomy and showing it the place which belongs to it in the hierarchy of life, then the two could really work in unison and bring about a saner and healthier world. But this will be an impossible task to accomplish, for the flow of time just cannot be reversed except through a process of 'charismatic resurrection'.[36]

That modernity is the natural trajectory of history and by the same token the destiny of tradition, and hence there should be no conflict between the two as such, is, another familiar argument. However, the theory of social change that sustains this argument, fails to explain how societies can change without losing their identity. Another flaw in the theory is that by standardising social change, it not only reduces it to a process of mechanical mimesis but also robs man of his intelligence, creativity and freedom. If we have "to imagine mankind pursuing a single way of life" as Levi-Strauss said "mankind would be ossified".[37]

It is unfortunate indeed that the successor to the traditional civilisation of India, the contemporary Indian society, instead of offering a creative response to the challenge of modernity, has been virtually behaving like a hungry body, subsisting upon its own reserves of energy — trying at times to revive its old traditions without understanding what they stand for and at others, to trace the dominant values of modernity to its own traditions. It is this pathological state which is the breeding ground of disvalues like nepotism, casteism, communalism and religious fundamentalism, which, contrary to the prevailing impression, are not the values of the traditional society, but disvalues synthesised by a sick society unable to face the challenge of modernity in a creative way. And hence the urgency to hark back to Gandhi who had shown the way to renaissant change.

## NOTES AND REFERENCES

1. We owe this phrase to Gilbert Ryle : *The Concept of Mind* (Penguin Books 1963).
2. Weber's concept of rationality in this context refers to 'substantive' and not to 'formal (purposive-instrumental) rationality' which, contrary to the expectations of Enlightenment cannot lead to the realisation of freedom; but can, only create an iron cage of bureaucratic rationality from which there will be no escape. (Bernstein R. Habermas and Modernity (1985) : Oxford, quoted by Harvey, David : 'The Condition of Postmodernity' : An Enquiry into the Origins of Cultural Change : Oxford, Basil Blackwell 1989, p. 15). Durkheim's concept of rationality is again slightly different from that of Pareto. While the former like Weber's is tempered with moral considerations, the latter stands for unmixed instrumental rationality.
3. Kant Immanuel : *Critique of Pure Reason* (London J.M. Dent and Sons 1950) p. 49.
4. See for example, Daya Krishna : *Considerations Towards a Theory of Social Change* (Bombay, P.C. Manaktala and Sons, Pvt. Ltd.; 1965) p. 130.
5. See especially Sri Aurobindo : Heraclitus (Calcutta, Arya Publishing House, College Street. Also, Zimmer, H : *The Philosophies of India*. ed. Joseph Campbell (New York, Meredian Books, 1956) Chap. IV and Rene Guenon : *Man and His Becoming according to Vedant* (New York, The Noonday Press, 1958).

6. Nisbet, Robert A : *Social Change and History* (New York, Oxford University Press, 1970) p. 36.
7. *ibid.* p. 37.
8. *ibid.* p. 39.
9. *ibid.* p. 23.
10. One day of *Brahma* is equal to one thousand cycles of development and decay in the Indian tradition. One cycle consists of four aeons representing full, three-fourths, half, and one-fourth of *Dharma* or order respectively in the descending order. The shortest in duration is the last aeon known as *Kali*, of which the ascending aeons are respectively twice, thrice, and four times as much in duration as *Kali*. The four aeons taken together make one cycle or one *Mahayuga*; and a thousand such cyclcs or *Mahayugas* constitute a *Kalpa* which is one day of Brahma the Creator. Each *Kalpa* is divided into fourteen *Manvantaras*, each ruled by a Manu (See especially, Hienerich Zimmer (1953) : *Myths and Symbols in Indian Art and Civilisation* (New York, Bollingen Series, Pantheon Books), Chapter I.
11. *Structural Sociology* in *Theoretical Sociology* ed., McKinney and Tiryakian, Edward A (New York Meredith Corporation, 1970) p. 126.
12. Parsons, Talcott: Societies, (Englewood Cliffs, New Jersey Prentice-Hall, Foundation of Modern Sociology Series, 1966).
13. The so-called 'dependency theory' of development was put forward by the Latin American intellectuals as an alternative to the prevailing 'modernisation' model which as the advocates of the theory argued was skewed in favour of the affluent as against the poor nations. The theory inspite of its Marxist facade was, as we argue, also a species of the modernisation model.The fact that we have also chosen to borrow the same terminology to enforce our argument need not mean any commitment on our part to the theory.
14. After the collapse of the USSR the globe has, as it is said, become unipolar. But considering the existing gap between the rich and the poor countries, re-emergence of a middle block in between the two which may revive the old distinction between the First, Second and Third World is not totally ruled out . There is a growing volume of opinion that what failed in Russia was not Marxism or Communism, but Stalinism, a system characterised not only by one person's rule, but by a hierarchically organised control of all aspects of social life, political, economic and cultural by a narrow oligarchy, seated at the apex of the party apparatus"(Callinicos A. : *The Revenge of History: Marxism and East European Revolution* (Cambridge Polity Press, 1991) p. 15, In : David Held: *Libaralism, Marxism and Democracy in Theory and Society*, Volume 22, April 1993), p. 261.
15. Benda, Julien : *The Betrayal of Intellectuals trans Richard Aldington* (Boston : The Beacon Press 1955).
16. Rudolph, S.H. and I.L. : *The Modernity of Tradition : Political Development in India* (Chicago, 1967).
17. Singer, Milton : Modernisation or Traditionalisation? in : (Contributions to Indian Sociology, New Series V, 1967).
18. Srinivas, M.N. : *Caste in Modern India and other Essays* (Bombay, Asia Publishing House, 1962).
19. Illustrative examples are : Madan, T.N. : 'Study of Social Change' in Contemporary India', in *Studies in Social Change*, (eds) K.S. Mathur

et al. (Lucknow Ethnographic and Folk Culture Society, 1973).

Dube, S.C. : 'Formulating the Goals of Change,' in *Some Aspects of Social Change in India* edited by Kuppuswamy and Mehta (Delhi Sterling Publishers, 1968).

Singh, Y. : *Modernisation of Indian Tradition* (Delhi, 1973).

Mandlebaum David, G. : *Society in India*, Volume II (Bombay Popular Prakashan, 1972).

Some notable exceptions are : Tariq Banuri : Modernisation and its Discontents : A Cultural Perspective on the Theories of Development in Frederique Apffel Margin and Stephen A. Margin, (eds) : Dominating Knowledge, Development, Culture and Resistance, (Oxford, Clarendon Press, 1990) in Dallmayr, Fred : Modernisation and Post-modernisation : Whither India? Alternatives 17(1992) pp. 421-452. Banuri rejects what Focault would call "hegemonic panopticism" 'inherent in "western liberalism's method of binary opposition," 'that is in its hierarchical rather than dialectical correlation of modernity and tradition, of universality and contextuality.' Banuri argues "that many of the seemingly insoluble problems of today's world stem precisely from the implicit assumptions of a dichotomy and a hierarchy between the impersonal and personal spheres of culture and that in our search for solutions we need to replace this hierarchy with the notion of a tension or a dialectic between the two." Banuri's vision of the future in the Third World can be expressed in terms of 'decentralised polity, economy and society' (Dallmayr, Fred, *op.cit.*, pp. 441-42).

Nandi, Ashis, likewise, lays emphasis on the revitalisation of indigenous culture or cultural traditions in the face of relentless Westernisation and uniformisation of the World. For Nandy, development essentially means "expansion of the awareness of oppression in society", and awareness of resistance to oppression, in the Third World countries as a component of development, would involve resistance to modernity, in particular, to such concepts as "development, growth, history, science and technology" which have become not only 'new reasons' of the state, but mystification for new forms of violence and injustice". (Cultural Frames for Social Transformation : A Credo, Alternatives 12 1987 : 113-117 in Dallmayr, Fred *op.cit.* p. 442.

For Rajni Kothari also it is not the expansion of 'technocratic or managerial controls but liberating transformation which holds the key to development, liberating transformation referring to freedom and democracy in human affairs and the institutions that sustain it. Kothari favours a "strengthening of local self-government and an invigoration of indigenous cultures and grassroots movements, especially among marginalised groups". "Ethnicity and pride in indigenous cultures," as he points out "are a response — including reaction to the excesses of the modern project of shaping the whole of humanity (and its natural resource base) around three pivots of world capitalism, the state system and a "world culture" based on modern technology, a pervasive communication and information order and a "universalising" "educational system". (Rethinking Development, In Search of the Humane Alternatives : Delhi : Ajanta, 1989 : in Dallmayr *op.cit.* Kothari advocates an open-ended engagement among cultures and an agonal dialogue among people (*lokayan*) and engagement that alone in his opinion can pave the way to equal respect among religions and cultural groups and to an alternative world.

20. Myrdal, Gunnar : *Asian Drama* (Pelican Books, 1968) 3 voulmes and *Challenge of World Poverty* (Pelican Books, 1971).
21. See also Kapp, William K. : *Hindu Culture : Economic Development and Economic Planning in India* (Bombay, Asia Publishing House 1963) Kapp also attributes the retarded economic development of India to her traditional culture.
22. Sri Aurobindo : *The Foundations of Indian Culture* (Pondichery, Sri Aurobindo Ashram, 1959) p. 73.
23. The cry is heard in the form of 'post-modernity' or 'post-structuralism' as exemplified in the works of Nietsche, Heidegger, Foucault, not least Habermas. Habermas has full faith in the self-correcting potentialities of reason and hence his tough resistence to the acceptance of any theory of 'post-modernity' or 'post-structuralism' as an extension of the project of Enlightenment. But neither 'communicative rationality' the new potential of Enlightenment reason discovered by him nor his concept of 'communicative competence' grounded thereon, nor again his theory of 'generalisability of norms', whereby Habermas seeks to resolve the dichotomy of 'fact', and 'value' can emancipate modernity from its the self-stultifying logic. Likewise the project of post-modernity or post-structuralism, — the manner in which it has been conceived, is bound to end up as nihilism as has actually happened. (See, Habermas Jurgen : *The Philosophical Discourse of Modernity*, trans, F. Lawrence (Cambridge, Mass MIT Press 1987) Towards a Theory of Communicative Competence, Enquiry 13, p. 360 65.
24. Mills, C. Wright : *The Sociological Imagination* (New York, Oxford University Press 1959).
25. Barzun, Jaques : *The House of Intellect* (New York Harper and Bros, 1959).
26. Marcuse, Herbert : *The One Dimensional Man* (London, Routledge and Kegan Paul, 1964).
27. See for example, Beteille, Andre : *Studies in Agrarian Social Structure* (Delhi, Oxford University Press, 1974).
28. Alternative theories of development such as those advanced by left-wing intellectuals like A. Gunder Frank do not move out of the duality which they consider as the Achilles heel of the received theories, the duality implicit in the assumption that development is either trasformation of a poor economy and society into another, supposed to be developed, or acculturation of a traditionally stagnant, immobile and underdeveloped society into a modern one through a diffusion of knowledge, skills, values technology etc. by its modern western counterpart. By attributing separate social structures to the developed and developing countries, the received theories split the structural whole into two and thus ignore the role played by it in creating the duality of wealth and poverty. We have no quarrel with scholars like Gunder Frank as far as their rejection of the numerous versions of the official theory is concerned. For our part, we find precious little to choose between one or the other version of the theory, if development according to it means carrying out the project of modernisation as a promotion of European rationality. Gunder Franks' suggestion that an alternative theory of development "must reflect the structure

and development of the system, which has given rise to, now maintains, and still increases both structural development and structural underdevelopment as simultaneous and mutually produced manifestations of the same historical process" (See his Latin America Underdevelopment or Revolution, New York and London 1970) again does not lead us anywhere beyond the point that the official theory in its actual implementation produces both development and underdevelopment simultaneously, a point which cannot be accepted within the framework of the normal theory of development to which we subscribe. The official theory according to our understanding can neither lead to development nor underdevelopment but only to a battle of ideologies over what development is and what it is not. For once an attempt is made to quantify development, there will be as many models or theories of development as there will be objectified goals of development. For instance, minimum needs, standard of living, quality of life etc. the principal ingredients of the hedonistic calculus in terms of which development is sought to be measured, can be defined or objectified in innumerable ways.

The world, in other words, to which a model of development will resemble will be its own projection; anything that the model fails to represent, will be eliminated from its scope. The literary archetype of modern development is to be found in the feat accomplished by Goethe's, epic hero Faust who "prepared to destroy religious myths, traditional values and customary ways of life in order to build a brave new world out of the ashes of the old, is in the end a tragic figure. Synthesising thought and action, Faust forces himself and everyone else (even Mephistopheles) to extremes of organisation, pain and exhaustion, in order to master nature and to create a new landscape, a sublime spiritual achievement that contains the potentiality for human liberation from want and need. Prepared to eliminate everything and everyone who stands in the way of realisation of this sublime vision, Faust, to his own ultimate horror, deploys Mephistopheles to kill a much-loved old couple who live in a small cottage by the sea shore for no other reason, than the fact that they do not fit in with the master plan". "It appears" says Berman "that the very process of development as it transforms the wasteland into a thriving physical and social space, recreates the wasteland inside the developer himself. This is how the tragedy of development works' (See Harvey, David : *The Condition of Postmodernity : An Enquiry into the Origins of Cultural Change.* Basil Blackwell Oxford, 1989) p. 16.

29. Friere, Paulo : *Cultural Action for Freedom*, Pedagogy of the Oppressed (Penguin Education, 1973).

30. Madhok, Balraj : *Indianisation* (New Delhi; Orient Paper Backs, 1970).

Archaism is a term used by Toynbee, Arnold J. to describe the mentality of the people who try to take refuge in the past to overcome the sickness resulting from the schism in the soul of a decadent civilisation. Futurists are the people who similarly try to live in the future, to escape from the present. Archaists may be fundamentalists also, people who mistake the truth of their myth as historical and act accordingly. (See his A Study of History, Abridgement of Volumes I-VII by Somerville D.C. London, Oxford University Press) pp. 375-376.

31. For a fuller understanding of this meaning of 'intellect', see, Schuon,

Frithjof : *The Transcendent Unity of Religions* (London, Faber and Faber, Ltd.).

32. Contrary to the impression created by Ashis Nandy and Fred Dallmayr what they call "critical traditionalism" is not a synthesis of tradition and modernity, but only a method of exploiting traditional material for bolstering up modern social institutions. For, tradition and modernity have their own distinct languages of discourse which cannot be rendered into each other. Tapping the 'liberating potential in tradition and combining it with its counterpart in modernity, will not be possible unless tradition could be reduced to a mere rehearsal of modernity. In which case, it would, be meaningless to speak of 'critical traditionalism'. Nor was Gandhi a 'critical traditionalist' or a 'marginalist' in this sense. (See Dallmayr Fred, *op.cit.* 421-452 and also his Margins of Political Discourse (University of New York Press Albony, 1989).

33. The traditional village communities provide the nearest example of a local polity based on unanimity and participatory democracy, communities which are facing extinction all over the world today in the wake of increasing political homogenisation. In the USA there is a strong movement, for populist politics and revitalisation of communities, to undo the excesses of modern spectacular politics ('which requires the prepackaging of whatever political issue is advocated to fit the media form' and "in which mainly intellectuals and lawyers pretending to represent virtue, goodness, beauty and the American way", participate, instead of the people at large). Populist politics aims at developing institutions which will ensure the growth of truly democratic politics based on face to face interaction of the people. "This does not mean politics understood in the sense of Enlightenment ideology gone mad, .... but the establishment of an adequate mode of representation, and expression of what is irreducibly private and its public otherness which integrates it within a social whole". Restructuring of communities likewise implies restoring to them their "particularly, specificity and otherness getting erased as a result of social homogenisation. (See Telos, November 87, Spring 1991 : *The Empire Strike out : Roundtable on Popular Politics*, Kenneth Anderson Russel A Berman, Tim Lake, Paul Piccone, and Michael Tanes.) pp. 6-7.

34. Fordism is the name of the organisational and technological innovations initiated or perfected by Henry Ford in America in the beginning of the twentieth century which not only boosted production, but resulted in the creation of a new type of worker and a new type of man. "What was special about Ford (and what ultimately separates Fordism from Taylorism), was his vision, his explicit recognition that mass production, meant mass consumption, a new system of reproduction of labour power, a new politics of labour control and management, a new aesthetic and psychology, in short, a new kind of rationalised and populist democratic society". (Harvey David, *op.cit.*, pp 125-126).

35. Schumacher pleads for "a new orientation of science and technology, towards the organic, the gentle, the non-violent, the elegant and the beautiful. "What he expects from science and technology is to provide us with methods and equipment :

- cheap enough so that they are accessible to virtually everyone,

— suitable for small scale application; and

— compatible with man's need for creativity.

Consistently with his stand, Schumacher recommends a decentralised system of production (not mass production but production for the masses) based on an intermediate/appropriate technology. There is much in Schumacher's economic philosophy to commend itself. He wants economics to be grounded in traditional wisdom, comes very close to Gandhi in his espousal of the philosophy of non-violence, non-stealing and non-acquisitiveness. But we have our own doubts if Schumacher's formula can go any way towards cutting modern science and technology down to size and bringing about the intended revolution in values. (Schumacher, E.F.: *Small is Beautiful* (Rupa & Co. paper back 1990), p. 27.

36. See especially Sorokin Pitirim, *The Crisis of Our Age?* (New York E.P. Dutton and Co. Inc., 1942)

37. See Kebede, Messay on the Relationship between the Spiritual and the Material : *The Lessons of Underdevelopment.* (Diogenes Number 162 Volume 41/2 1993) p. 122.

TWO

# SOCIAL POLICY AND THE CHALLENGE OF POST-INDUSTRIAL TRANSFORMATION

ANANTA GIRI

## The Problem

For the last two decades, advanced industrial societies have been undergoing fundamental transformation in their social, economic, political and cultural domains. The ongoing process of this transformation is leading to the emergence of a new type of society whose full contours are yet to emerge. The trends of this emergent formation are looked at as part of "The Coming of the Post Industrial Society" (Bell, 1973). Along with the change from a predominantly industrial, manufacturing economy to a hi-tech and service economy, this transformative process has entailed some curious and shocking changes in the politics, administrative policy and culture in advanced capitalist societies. The post-war faith in the principles of "Welfare State" has yielded to a redefinition of the priorities of state and society. Social policy in advanced capitalist societies in North America and Europe has turned increasingly "consrervative" in the last decade. This reorientation is being justified as crucially necessary to confront the restructuring forces of post-industrialism and to instill dynamism and innovation to an otherwise lethargic and bureaucratic system (Dahrendorf, 1988).

In this realm of ongoing post-industrial transformation, the process of which has many painful consequences such as "deindutrialisation", "unemployment", "under-employment", low-paying service job, what is to be the guiding principle and philosophy of a social policy? What is the role of State and different institutions in confronting the challenge of late capitalism? How and in which direction do the existing social policies have to be transformed in order to cope with the challenge of post-industrial transformation? Answer to these historically significant questions for survival require a critical reflection on the challenge of the post-industrial transformation and the accompanying need for transforming the theory and practice of social policy.

## Post-Industrial Transformation and Contemporary Restructuring

The "Great U-Turn" that the post-industrial transformations has led to is best reflected in the domain of contemporary economic restructuring. In advanced capitalist societies, the decline of the manufacturing sector and the ascendency of the service economies also witnessing fundamental restructuring of the location of industries, where high technology has enabled a flight of capital from the snowbelt to sunbelt and to the safe havens of the Third World villages. At the global realm, high technology makes possible the mergence of multinational corporations, a global assmebly line, a global restructuring of industrial activities and spatial forms creating a "global techno-structure of production, ... investment and trade" (Bright & Geyer, 1987). This globalisation of production, distribution and exchange has also been accompanying by the economic crisis of the advanced industrial countries in the 1970s (Cuomo, 1988; Goldthorpe, 1984). Moreover, this global and regional economic restructuring has also led to the spatial restructuring of the cities. Contemporary urban restructuring has been accompanied by the processes of "genetrification", "abandonment", and displacement, creating "new homelessness" and "hardship in heartland". This restructuring has also led to the rise of the post-industrial cities as competitive units in the global economy (Harvey, 1985; Sassem, 1988 & Savitch, 1988).

But contemporary economic restructuring is not simply confined to the manufacturing sector. Deindustrialisation is now being seen in the service sector as well; its victims are not solely the blue collar workers of Detroit and Pittsburg but also the company managers and professionals who are "falling from grace" in the wave of the post-industrial restructuring (Newman, 1988).

Post-industrial transformation is also restructuring the internal organisation of industries. Industries now require workers with advanced technical skills for which they have to go beyond the boundaries of "the internal labour market". "The new emphasis on high-skill work and well-trained labour is partly responsible for the recent decline in the role of the internal labour market and the increasing reliance of firms on the external labour market" (Noyelle, 1987 : 2). The rise of the informal economy is also restructuring the internal labour market of the firms (Portes et al. 1989). Part-time job has also devoluted the internal labour market. At the level of firm, high technology is also leading to a general regime of flexible accumulation, specialisation and exchange (Harvey, 1987; Piore & Sabel, 1984). As one commentator tells us; "Under vertical disintegration, firms tend to specialise in types of classes of production rather than in production of large quantities of specific outputs as in mass production. The essence of the firm becomes flexible production" (Noyelle, 1987 : 101).

Contemporary economic restructuring also manifests itself in a cataclysmic rise in speculative economic activity and flight from responsible assessment of risks. The economic crisis that the post-industrial transformation has created is an integral part of the coming of the "casino society" and the rise of "paper enterpreneurialism" (Bluestone & Harrison, 1988 : 63). Now it has been cheaper to acquire another company and its entire capital stock than to invest in new plant and equipment. In this encessant merger and acquisitions, new technologies also make possible the growth of corporate megastructures. But as anthropologist Marvin Harris (1981) rightly points out, the spell and appeal of particular products are also lost in such faceless merger and acquisitions which for him is one of the crucial reasons for the losing ground of American products in the global market.

The economic crisis of the postindustrial transition has also given rise to fundamental political restructuring in late capitalism. The most visible development here is the rise of the New Right and its attack on the Welfare State on grounds of its inefficiency as well as the current fiscal crisis. The conservative counter-revolution has supposedly come up to throw government off the back of the people and unleash their creativity and initiative to make the most and the best of the post-industrial opportunity. This political restructuring seems all pervasive : even in the exceptional case of Sweden, there have been new divisions and anti-solidaristic strategies (Offe, 1988 : 217). But this political restructuring has taken place in the context of the restructuring of class and the "destructuration of collectivities" (Offe, 1988 : 215). Here, as Offe tells us : "the primary significance rests with new forms of structural and cultural plurality leading to the virtual evaporation of classes and other self-concious collectivities of political will...." (Offe, 1988 : 218). What Stuart Hall writes about Thatcherism makes clear the total revolution that this political restructuring strives to bring:

> "Politically, Thatcherism is related to the recomposition and 'fragmentation' of the historic relations of representation between state and civil society, 'public' and 'private', the emergence of new arenas of contestation, new sites of social antagonism, new social subjects and political identities in contemporary society" (Hall, 1988 : 2).

But this conservation revolution and political restructuring have not been made possible solely due to image manipulation and conspiracy since, as Hall argues. "In and through images, fundamental political questions are being posed and argued through" (Hall, 1988 : 261). The challenge here is to understand the structural foundations behind the dissatisfaction with welfare state and liberal democratic forces operated with the assumption that the expansion of the welfare state is in the best interests of the common people. "Post-war social democrats always talked in terms of the enabling and facilitating states and never explicitly faced the empirical evidence that the interests of the state — its officials and politicians — were in opposition to those of ordinary citizen" (Ignatieff, 1989 : 69). When liberal forces not only defended the welfare state but also struggled for its massive expansion, "The New Right presented itself as the only party committed to oppose the exponential growth of the state ..." (Hall, 1988 : 227). But we have to realise that the New Right did not invent the dissatisfaction with the state in the first place.

It is undoubtedly true that the economic crisis of the welfare state which has generated individualistic political attitude and orientations has translated into a political crisis of the welfare state. But was this translation inevitable and unavoidable? Claus Offe argues that "in all such cases, the decisive change occurs not only on the level of objective events but on the level of interpretative framework ..." (Offe, 1988 : 215) in the context of post-industrial crisis, the New Right was successful in providing an ideological alternative to the destructuration and ambiguity of post-industrialism.

Questioning the argument of the inevitability of the conservative retrenchment of the welfare state enables us to understand the complex process in which anti-welfare retrenchment has actually operated. Here it is crucial to realize that the beneficiaries of the welfare state are "Not only the Poor" (Goodin & Grand, 1987), but also the middle classes who have a crucial role in creating, expanding, reforming and dismantling the welfare state, "the middle classes had significant interests in its preservation, interests neither politicians nor civil servants could safely ignore" (Grand & Winter, 1987 : 148). In Sweden, even the bourgeoisie coalition has not detracted from the philosophy and practice of welfare state (Fry, 1979 : 7).

But political restructuring in post-industrial society is not simply confined to reactive and defensive mobilizations, but also includes those movements who are mobilizing for restructuring of the relationship between political party, civil society and citizens and the rise of grass-roots "critical social movements" as the agents of people's "need interpretation" (Fraser, 1987). These social movements are agents of "self-production" (Youraine, 1977) and historicity in programmed societies where "society's work upon itself is no longer carried only in the economic order but almost always in the domains of culture" (Touraine, 1981 : 73). Touraine tells us : "In post-industrial society, social movement from around what is called consumption in the name of personal collective identity, yet at the heart of the great apparatus of production and management — not in relation to the system of ship" (Touraine, 1977 : 323). The movements "contest the administrative logic of the social state as they struggle for the power interpret their members' needs and to institute democratic, dialogue and empowering communicative relations" (Fraser, 1987 : 31).

The restructuring process of post-industrialism is not simply confined to economy and politics it is also restructuring "the script of life in modern society and the boundaries of culture. According to Bunchman, "Unemployment due to structural (technological) change or economic factors undermine the "life long" integration in the occupational system that has characterized male occupational careers since Second World War. Thus, the individual's movement through the occupational system is gradually losing its highly standardised form" (Buchman, 1989 : 48). Moreover, "The rapidly decreasing half-life of the usability of acquired expertise gives rise to short-term work perspectives and induces a relatively low degree of calculability and predictability". Hence, post-industrial transformation not only creates a flexible specialization on the shop floor, but also engenders a flexible lifecourse. Fred Block makes this restructuring of the lifecourse very clear : "The patterns of social life consolidated in this country after twenties and thirties continued to organize people's lives around measured labour time, the basis of the old productive forces ... aspects of this organisation of social life have been undermined by the progressive emergence of new productive forces over the past fifty years" (Block, 1987 : 109). Because of part-time work, informal economy and the home work, the relationship between work-time, non-work time and leisure is changing. "This interpretation of time structure leads to the reorganization of time in the entire life course" (Buchman, 1989 : 57).

But as in the case of political restructuring, this restructuring of the lifecourse is not simply a reaction formation to the sweeping forces of post-industrialism. In the domain of the post-industrial life-world, there has also occurred the development of a post-modern self, which embodies a "post-individualist" "charismatic reaction to the contradiction between formal and substantive rationality embodied in the modern self" Studies show that contemporary professionals have a process orientation towards themselves in relation to organisation rather than a product orientation. The post-modern self has emerged in the context of the rise of the post-modern culture. Post-modern culture is accompanied by the destructuration of the great summarizing discourse and the rise of local narratives and local knowledge. "Post-modernism is reflected in the post-Marxist socialist politics of the 'new social movements' or 'socialist pluratism. It expresses itself in Foucault's micro-macro politics and the new politics of localities" (Graham, 1988 : 61). The emerging cultural sensibility in the contemporary "condition of postmodernity" (Harvey, 1989) is striving to transcend the institutional and discursive boundaries of modernity and to imagine, explore and create alternative space in the contemporary landscape of despair.

## Post Industrial Challenges and the Imperative for Policy Transformation

The overwhelming and all-encompassing restructuring that post-industrial transformation has brought urgently calls for a transformation in our weltaschauung and in our social policy. The logic of post-industrialism makes it inevitable transformations in social policy and in social institutions in order that the entry into the post-industrial world does not degenerate solely into disruption and dislocation. Post-industrial transformation has engendered crisis in existing social organisation and representation. But it also has the potential of a renewal and reorganization of individual and society, the realization of which requires a transformation in self, institution and social policy.

## Need for Institutional Transformation

In coping with the challenge of post-industrial transformation and directing its restructuring towards a more humane social order, we have to realize that economic crisis is part of a larger social crisis and cannot be solved through simple economic alterations, such as change in the budget allocation. Rather it calls for the growth of new social institutions and the development of a radically new social policy. Fred Block articulates very clearly the imperatives for a transformed social policy in contemporary restructuring :

> "... Post-industrial developments place institutional problems at the centre of the policy agenda. Traditional macro-economic policies were purely quantitative increasing aggregate demand, slow the growth of the money supply, reduce taxes —but these measures fail to address the new problems. The new problems are institutional; how can firms be organised to make maximal productive use of human skills and technological advances; how can services like health care and education—which constitute a growing share of total consumption expenditures —be organised most effectively; how can we devise mechanisms for deciding about the allocation of capital to infrastructure development —transportation, energy, communications —in a situation where neither the market nor centralised planning has proven its effectiveness" (Block, 1987 : 28-29).

Post-industrial transformation makes it imperative the establishment of a regime of flexible accumulation and specialization which, in turn, depends on "the creation of institutions that resolve the micro - and macro-economic problems along new technological trajectories" (Piore & Sabel, 1984 : 263). In post-industrial societies flexible specialisation is better able to accommodate the fluctuations in exchange rates and commodity process than in a regime of mass-production. But there is an inherent incompatibility between the existing hierarchical and Taylorist forms of work organization and the operation of new technologies in the regime of flexible specialization. Advanced technologies have not only lead to fundamental spatial and economic restructuring is post-industrial societies, they also make urgent a restructuring of work organisations. The new technologies of computer and micro electronics are rapidly transforming the nature of work. But new technologies in many different realm — from the work place to genetic counselling — have been used as an instrument in the control of workers and ordinary people. However, new technologies also have a more non-hierarchal and democratizing potential.

Post-industrial development also necessitates the building up of a post-industrial built-environment and social infrastructure which, in turn, makes it urgent a transformation in the existing relationship between state and society. The post industrial social infrastructure can not be built in the current social policy of retrenchment and general austerity. "Similarly, generalised austerity with the resulting decline in the physical and themental health of the population would undermine the capacity of organizations to expand the learning components of jobs" (Block, 1987 : 125). Moreover, wihout the accompanying policy transformation and institutional development to appropriate new productive forces, old forms of exploitation are intensified. The contemporary trend of high tech and low pay is a case in point.

Post-industrial change not only makes it imperative a reconceptualization of disadvantage in the social policy agenda, it also calls for a critical rethinking of the appropriateness of the foundational assumptions of existing social policies. American social policy is built on a bifurcation between social security and public assistance. This bifurcation has, in turn, created two different representations of the beneficiaries of social policy : the citizens and the clients. "Social security by the stably employed majority of citizens has become by the 1960s institutionally and symbolically separated from welfare for the barely deserving poor" (Weir et al., 1988 : 26). Moreover, the New Deal welfare system in U.S. was based upon commercial Keynesianism, not on social needs of the American workers" (Skocpol, 1988 : 302). It gives rise to compensatory welfare which ultimately helped in regulating the poor, rather than empowering them. In this context, the Reagan "Means Season" represents an "understandable culmination of the original failure of the New Deal to institutionalise social Keynesian policies...." (Skopol, 1988 : 302). Even the Great Society Program of President Johnson did not transcend this New Deal bifurcation between social security and social welfare.

**Transforming the State**

The imperative for a transformed social policy that post-industrialism heightens is no where more urgent than in the transformation of the State. The task of building a transformed social infrastructure to cope with the post-industrial challenge can be accomplished neither by the free market nor by the centralised state. Post-industrial societies are characterized by collective goods as opposed to public goods which not only presage a sharp rise in political conflict but also call into question the structure of government institutions themselves (Benjamin, 1980). The rise of the collective goods brings the question of a generalised social welfare and raises the question whether these collective goods are best delivered by centralised and bureaucratic institutions.

But the necessity for the increasing role of the government is not to be confused with the perpetuation of the bureaucratic and the corporatist state. What post-industrialism needs is a renewal, revitalisation and transformation of state. As Marc Levine et al. writes : ". . . time has come to revitalize the notion of a progressive, democratic state in the United States" (1988 : 2). But they make clear what they mean when they advocate for a revitalized government : "This is not a book about statism. We are not advocates of stifling, centralised, and essentially undemocratic bureaucracies". The policy change that the post-industrial transformation necessitates calls for the liberation, identity and dignity" (Kothari, 1988 : 7).

The imperative for policy change that the coming of the

post-industrial society creates challenges us to design an appropriate social policy that is capable of transforming the dislocation of post-industrialism into a source of total renewal and reorganization of self and society. Social policy designed for post-industrial society has to strive for creating a "post-bureaucratic" society. Social policy has to facilitate the growth of post-Taylorist and post-Weberian forms of organisation both in the workplace as well as in other domains of social administration. Block argues : "One of the signposts of post-industrial change are the efforts by corporations to devise new forms of organisation that diverge sharply from classical Weberian bureaucracies" (Block, 1987 : 29). Various companies are developing work groups instead of hierarchies. "The new bureaucracy" in contemporary advanced capitalist societies is characterised by managerial self-renewal (Skertchy, 1977 : 289) and "fewer levels of supervision, diminished deferences to hierarchical authority, greater reliance on teamwork, and expanded decision-making responsibilities for lower-level employees" (Block, 1987 : 29). For Block the emergent "post-bureaucratic organisations are more effective than traditional bureaucracies in situations where changing technologies and changing markets create high levels of uncertainity and unpredictibility" (Block, 1987 : 29).

Service delivery, in the welfare system as well as in other areas, also has to be post-bureaucratic. In many instances, social movements among the welfare recipients have instilled the energy and dynamism of the lifeworld into the system world of the welfare bureaucracy and have transformed the clients from their undifferentiated passivity to a political constituted collectivity. Citizen movements, citizen groups and voluntary organizations present themselves not only as alternative agents of people's need interpretation but also as alternative agents of service delivery. Here, rethinking in social service delivery in post-industrial societies provides a model for designing an appropriate social policy.

Social policy in creating a post-bureaucratic society can also derive inspiration from the recent initiative in 'taming the bureaucracy' by the government and the citizen movements (Gromley, 1989) in the past decades. The recent efforts in taming the bureaucracy, as William Gromley Jr. tells us, have involved both strategies of coercive and catalytic controls, both muscle and prayers. Each strategy has its own advantage though the strategy of prayer helps in creating a creative democracy. When the buraucrate know which interests they want to represent, but don't know which policies they ought to pursue. "Prayers make lot of sense . . . prayers may encourage self-actualization and discourage pork barrel politics. A final advantage is that prayer promote bureaucratic creativity, flexibility, innovation, and experimentation" (Gromley, 1989 : 231).

## A Positive Government

The idea of a "positive government" (Cuomo, 1988) is central to the design of an appropriate social policy for the post-industrial society. In the post-industrial economy, the government has to provide leadership in creating an ethos for production and productive investment in a "casino" climate of speculation and merger. "The fundamental issues of the 1990s will be economic (Osborne, 1988 : 20). But the economic problem of contemporary advanced capitalist societies is not simply produced by the macro-economic disequilibrium of forces (Cuomo, 1988 : 21). "In the last analysis, what matters is production" (Cuomo, 1988 : 31). But in this challenging domain, 'more than the federal governments, states have taken steps to meet them" (Cuomo, 1988 : 107). Many states in the U.S. have already launched such partnership ventures which R. Kanter so aptly characterises as 'Investment Economics and the politics of Partnership" (Kanter, 1988). Here rather than targeting specific industries or products, most states are targeting processes : technological innovation and Capital formation.

In post-industrial societies, capital formation for investment is problematic and here state initiatives are important. The existing financial institutions are not meeting the need for capital on the part of the small business and other social groups. Perhaps for this reason, Michael Dukakis as Governor of Massachussetts, had created many quasi-public finance agencies. The Massachussetts Housing Partnership, a distinguished board of forty public and private groups, is a case in point. Governor Jim Blanchard of Michigan has also established a Michigan Venture Capital Fund to assist in the economic revitalisation of the cities abandoned by deindustrialisation. These state developmental initiatives are comprehensive but decentralised. These programmes are local, "they have the capacity to make decisions quickly, the flexibility to respond to a wide variety of problems, and the credibility that can only be earned through the daily contact with the people" (Osborne, 1988 : 261). Such investment economics and the politics of partnership help in the recovery of communities and cities, hard hit by post-industrial restructuring. Because of Ben Franklin Partnership even Pittsburg, hard hit by the decline of the steel industry, is remarkably well positioned for the high-tech economy of the future.

**Welfare and Efficiency**

Two crucial agendas in the post-industrial societies are : creating economic growth and bringing the poor into the growth process. Governments have to play an interventionalist role in both these two domains. Governments can stimulate production by promulgating an investment tax credit 'tailored to encourage investment in new process of technology and equipment" (Cuomo, 1988 : 121). It has to build a solid educational infrastructure by creating post-industrial universities and making education a lifelong process on the part of workers in particular and people in general. In the regime of flexible specialisation, the urgent "task is to develop community-based approaches to social and economic problems" (Osborne, 1988 : 13). Governments have to create partnership banks and companies which would invest in private public partnerships that would assume a longer-time horizon. There must be national standards for social spending and revenue sharing coupled with national economic policies that provide for full employment (Carnoy et al., 1983 : 209). In late capitalism, the state has spent a disproportionate amount of its energy and enthusiasm in armament production. But an appropriate social policy designed for post-industrial societies requires 'a well-planned expansion of the public sector in non-military areas' (Carnoy et al., 1983 : 160).

Here the challenge is to create a broad-based political support for the argument that a transformed social welfare policy that enables people to cope with structural disadvantage and creates opportunities for education and mobility is in the best interests of a prosperous economy. Global competitiveness has become a major issue for many economies in advanced capitalist countries and a reformed social welfare system would enhance the competitive positions of the troubled economies such as contemporary American economy. As Block argues : "Greater employment and income security, more democracy at the workplace, greater option for adult education and training, more extensive family and community services, and more flexible working time are also aspects of a post-industrial transformation of work that would make the economy more efficient" (Block, 1987 : 154).

Flexibility is the key word in the post-industrial transition and social policy designed to cope with its challenge must strive towards the institutionalisation of a flexible lifecourse. To cope with the deindustrialisation of post-industrialism, it seems that early retirement to ensure full employment is more in the right direction. This has already become a major concern of social policy in Western Europe ..." (Block, 1987 : 134). However, there needs to be a flexibility in the structuration between work-time, family time and non-work time. The flexibile restructuring of time in division of labour is also a demand of the New Christian Right in general and the pro-life movement in particular.

The particulars of an appropriate social policy are certainly important but what is much more crucial is developing a broad framework for policy analysis. Here the fundamental thrust of a post-industrial social policy has to be its comprehensiveness : targeting both the middle class and the lower class. This comprehensive social policy would enable individuals, groups and classes to cope with the growing polarisation of the post-industrial transition. This social policy has to be empowering, rather than compensatory. This empowering social policy in the post-industrial society has to create space for a dialogic "life World" (Hebermas, 1987) and has to make the ongoing "Return of the Actor" (Touraine, 1988) possible. The social policy assigned to cope with the challenge of postindustrial transformation has to implant a post-industrial theory of justice by making a creative balance among production, income and distribution.

**REFERENCES**

Bell, Daniel (1962) : *The End of Ideology*, Cambridge, Mass : Harvard University Press.

Bell, Daniel (1963) : *The Coming of the Post-Industrial Society*, NY : Basic Books.

Benjamin, Roger (1980) : *Collective Goods and Political Change in Post-Industrial Societies*, Chicago.

Block, Fred (1987) : *Revising State Theory : Essays in Politics and Post-Industrialism*, Temple.

Block, Fred et al. (1987) : *The Mean Season : The Attack on the Welfare State*, NY : Pantheon.

Bluestone, B. and B. Harrison (1988) : *The Great U-Turn : Corporate Restructuring of the Polarising of America*, NY : Basic Books.

Bright, Charles and M. Geyer (1987) : *For a Unified History in the Twentieth Century*, Ms.

Bunchman, Marlis (1989) : *The Script of Life in Modern Society : Entry into Adulthood in a Changing World*, Chicago.

Carnoy, Martin and D. Shearer (1980) : *Economic Democracy : The Challenge of the 1980s*, NY : ME Sharpe.

Cuomo, Mario (1988) : *The Coumo Commission Report on Competitiveness*, NY : Simon and Schuster.

Darhendorf, Rolf (1988) : Changing Values Under Mrs. Thatcher. In : *Thacharism* edited by R. Skidelsky, London : Charter & Windus.

Dukakis, Michael S. and R. Kanter (1988) : *Creating the Future : Massachussetts Comeback and its Promise for America*, NY : Summit Books.

Fraser, Nancy (1987) : *Social Movements vs Disciplinary Democracies : The Discourse of Social Needs*, Minnestota.

Fry, John. (ed.) (1979) : *Limits of the Welfare State : Critical Views on Post War Sweden*, London : Saxon House.

Goldthorpe, J.H. (ed.) (1984) : *Order and Conflict in Contemporary Capitalism*, Oxford.

Goodin, R. and J. Grand (eds.) (1987) : *Not only the Poor : The Middle Classes and the Welfare State*, London : Allen & Unwin.

Graham, Oullie (1988) : Post-modernism and Marxism, *Antipode* 20 (1), 60-66.

Gromley, William (1989) : *Taming the Bureaucracy : Muscle, Prayer and other Strategies*, Princeton.

Habermas, Jurgen (1987) : *The Theory of Communicative Action.* Vol. 2 : Life World and System, Cambridge, MIT Press.

Hall, Stuart (1988) : *The Hard Road to Renewal : Thatcherism and the Crisis of the Left*, London : Verso.

Harris, Marvin (1981) : *America Now : The Anthropology of a Changing Culture*, NY : Simon and Schuster.

Harvey, David (1985) : *Urbanisation of Capital*, Johns Hopkins.

Harvey, David (1987) : Flexible Accumulation Through Urbanisation Reflection on Post-modernism in American City, *Antipode* 19(3) : 260-286.

Harvey, David (1989) : The Condition of Post-modernity Basic Blackwell Hertz, S.

Ignatieff, Michael (1989) : Citizenship and Moral Narcissism. *The Political Science Quarterly*, 60(1) : 63-70.

Kothari, Rajni (1988) : *Transformation and Survival : The Search of the Humane World Order*, New Delhi : Ajanta.

Levine, Marc et al. (1988) : *The State and Democracy : Revitalising America's Government*, Roultedge.

Newman, Katherine (1988) : *Falling from Grace : The Experience of Downward Mobility in American Middle Class*, NY : Free Press.

Noyelle, Thierry (1987) . *Beyond Industrial Dualism : Market and Job Segmentation in the New Economy*, Boulder : Westview Press.

Piore, Michael and C. Sabel (1984) : *The Second Industrial Divide : Possibilities for Prosperity*, NY : Basic Books.

Portes, A. et al. (eds.) (1989) : *The Informal Economy : Studies in Advanced and Less Developed Societies*, Baltimore : The Johns Hopkins, U. Press.

Offe, Clause (1988) : Democracy Against the Welfare State? Structural Foundations of Neconservative Political Opportunities, In : J.D. Munn (ed.) *Responsibility Rights and Welfare : The Theory of the Welfare State* Boulder : Westview Press.

Osborne, David (1988) : *Laboratories of Democracy*. Boston : Harvard Business School.

Rochon, Thomas (1988) : *Mobilizing for Peace*. Princeton.

Seasen Seskia (1988) : *The Mobility of Capital and Labour*, Cambridge.

Savitch, H.V. (1988) : *Post-Industrial Cities*. Princeton.

Skerchly, A.R. (1978) : New Bureaucracy : Reconstruction of State Government Bureaucracies to meet the needs and expectations of the Post-Industrial Society, Perth, West Australia : Management Development.

Skoopol, Theda (1988) : Limits of the New Deal System and the Roots of Contemporary Welfare Dilemmas. In : Weir et al.

Touraine, Alain (1977) : *The Self Production of Society*, Chicago.

Touraine, Alain (1981) : *The Voice and the Bye*, Cambridge.

Touraine, Alain (1983) : *Anti-Nuclear Protest*, Cambridge.

**THREE**

# MAPPING FOR ENVIRONMENTAL MANAGEMENT AND SUSTAINABLE DEVELOPMENT

L.R.Singh

## I

Sustainable development has acquired the popularity of a catchword which is used by the political leaders, environmentalists, economists and social planners in their own way often without reference to a substantive context and a coherent conceptual framework. In fact its varied usages evince concerns for impending crises and dangers of development processes which seldom help in promoting economic dynamism, social equity and ecological stability.

The concept of 'sustainable development' was first introduced in the World Conservation Strategy in 1980 in the context of appropriate technology and energy conservation and gained its currency in Our Common Future, Report of the U.N. World Commission on Environment and Development, published in 1987. It was well reflected in the deliberations of the Earth Summit held at Rio in June, 1992. It has different connotations in the spatio-temporal framework. "Every citizen on earth wants his or her environment used and managed in a sustainable manner. But the divided economic conditions force different environmental management objectives on different nations and communities. While the rich and well-fed are more interested in the environment because they want to secure their future, the poor and dispossessed, caught in a daily struggle to survive, are more interested in the environment because they want to secure their present".[1]

There are wide disparities in development of the developed industrialised nations and the developing nations of the world as revealed by the World Development Report for 1992. It recognized the vital links between economic development and environment. The differential patterns reflect variations in economic, social and ecological conditions and approaches :

1. "Environmental problems in developing countries largely result from a great stress on the natural base (for example, over-exploitation of ground-water and surface water, land degradation, deforestation, etc.) whereas environmental problems in industrialised countries largely result from problems of pollution and disposal of waste".
2. "Environmental management in industrialised countries can afford to take a conservation approach with respect to land, water and forests. In developing countries, given the extreme pressures on the natural resource base for daily survival, on the one hand, and economic growth, on the other, and a rational and sustainable resource exploitation will be able to reconcile environmental constraints with development requirements. But trade-offs can be carefully considered in poor economies and a long-term view adequately incorporated if they can generate more than what they need for current consumption. In other words they need adequate financial resources for sustainable development".[2]

That is why Mike Young has argued for sustainable investment for sustainable development because if environmental quality and ecological integrity are to be maintained "amongst other things, investment will have to be coupled to ecosystem and environmental requirements and decoupled from environmental degradation".[3]

Development is no more a synonym for growth and the expansion of the G.N.P., an important indicator of development of a country, does not necessarily promote sustainable development which should be better measured in terms of a sustainable increase in real per capita income over a period of time.[4] "Growth should be such as to provide meaningful work, a reasonable minimum standard of living and essential social amenities to everyone as speedily as possible. It should also be more sensitive to the needs of the disadvantaged and vulnerable while also making for a more wide-spread diffusion of the benefits of development across regions and classes than has been achieved so far".[5] In fact 'economic growth has been accompanied by neglect and degradation of the environment and uncontrolled exploitation of natural resource base' and has thus jeoparadised the basis for sustainable development, which must improve the quality of life[6] and living environment in both qualtitative and qualitative terms on a continuous basis. That is way the U.N. World Commission on Environment and Development has defined sustainable development as "development that meets the needs of the present without compromising the ability of future generations to meet their own needs". It certainly conceives of sustainability of ecological and social systems rather than economic sustainability only.

Sustainability stands for survival which can be ensured by providing the basic human needs of food, shelter and clothing of evergrowing population and its spiraling demands by increased means of production and greater efficiency in production (e.g. 'Green Revolution", or 'Blue Revolution", 'Technological Innovation').

"Sustainability also means an ecologically acceptable production, where everything removed is then replaced so as not to harm the ecological system".[7] It is certainly a limiting factor because the level of production should be ecologically desirable and should be in tune with eco-cultural trusteeship which conceives of both utilisation and preservation of present and future generations.

Sustainability also implies social equity with reference to "production structures and relationships which ensure a fair distribution of income, power and opportunities thus providing the basis for social peace".[8]

Sustainable development can be achieved by maintaining environmental integrity, promoting economic efficiency and ensuring social equity at regional, national and international levels. Young has aptly remarked : "Sustainability is intimately connected with the issues of justice, rights and obligations. Beyond these broad ideas, attempts to present a single definition tend to be counter-productive. A sustainable future is dependent upon the retention of a diverse range of approaches and opinions about the best way to achieve sustainable development. Diversity is essential for successful evolution and that is what sustainability is about : encouraging and facilitating the evolution of social and economic activity in directions that improve the welfare of the present and future people".[9]

Although sustainable development is a laudable objective,

its achievement is illusive because of the several constraints. In the first instance there is no real acceptance of sustainability as a common goal by the government, industry and society. There is also lack of political will for implementing the programmes for sustainable development which impinge on vested interests. The limits to growth cannot be ignored if over-exploitation and degradation of the natural resource base is to be checked and environmental management is to be resorted to. Perhaps it will have to wait for a new social and economic order based on social well-being and ecological integrity.

## II

Map is an essential tool of geography. It unfolds the variegated vistas of the vast man-earth interacting system, divisible into myriad of sub-systems at national, regional and local levels. It is certainly a highly useful visual aid for the understanding and appreciation of national/regional diversities, differential levels of national/regional development, their problems and potentials. It can be used as an efficient tool for mapping sustainable development in specific spatio-temporal framework where symbiotic relationships between Place-Work-Folk should be delineated for the sustainability of the dynamic ecosystem that evolves due to interaction of environmental impact, human economy and social polity.

This view leads to the concept of eco-development which forms the core of sustainable development as it helps in charting the course and pattern of development in terms of ecological integrity and helps in balancing and harmonising various human enterprises for improving the quality of environment, quality of life and well-being, free from deleterious effects of external interferences. It visualises conservation, management and development of resources by appropriate technological base and institutional framework which ensure economic well-being and socio-cultural development of the local people.

These concerns for sustainable development can be visually expressed in maps which can focus on utilisation, conservation and development of natural and human resources on national and regional levels. They can portray their limitations and potentialities which can be used in planning for their optimum utilisation in terms of ecological integrity. They can be of great help in identifying and assessing environmental degradation, environmental hazards, sources of pollution, economic deprivation, social inequities and region-specific measures of the control and management.

In a large country like India with diverse resource patterns and regional differentials in development there is urgent need for building up a system of macro-meso and micro planning regions on the basis of detailed regional surveys of natural and human resources.[10] "The over-all strategy of economic development has to draw support and sustenance from regional studies of resources and possibilities, it must in turn give direction and balance to regional planning and reveal the impact of one development on many related aspects. In the absence of such studies covering the entire field, it would not be possible to guide development rationally, avoid costly mistakes and anticipate future contingencies wisely and constructively".[11] In such regional exercises the role of maps is very important for they singly and collectively express the spatial realities and spatial connectivities more eloquently and highlight the basic issues and guide the planners in taking rational and pragmatic decisions. Of course, the cartographer can make use of data available from air surveys, National Remote Sensing Agency and National Resource Data Management System. He has a difficult task of handling the plethora of data in a thematic manner and mapping it on the micro-regional scales for purposes of action plans.

Environmental planning is *sine qua non* for sustainable development. Environment is a complex whole or an ensemble of inter-related geo-elements which undergo transformation due to human activities in a spatio-temporal framework. Maps can faithfully represent these complex spatial realities and can prove of great help in environmental planning by diagnostic and prescriptive cartographic exercises. Mapping of natural hazards like floods, droughts, desertifications, cyclones, landslides, deforestation, soil erosion, waterlogging and wastelands provide good examples. Of course, their conservation, utilisation and development is fraught with serious technological, cultural and economic problems but this colossal loss/waste can be minimised by sustained planning efforts for promoting an environmentally sound development.

The detailed surveys of land utilisation, land capability and efficiency are urgently needed for agricultural planning which should be area-specific in terms of physico-biotic potential and eco-developmental needs. Maps provide a scientific system for preparation of land resource inventories and delineation of agricultural planning regions which are basically agro-climatic regions. They help in understanding correlations of geo-ecological conditions and cropping patterns and depict their spatio-temporal changes as caused by demographic pressure, technological transformation and institutional framework. They can highlight the problems of degradation of agricultural land or encroachment of traditional agriculture on marginal lands, pastures and forest land or usurpation of fertile agricultural land by non-agricultural uses.

Irrigation is an essential input for agricultural development but it is a mixed blessing because of its adverse effects (e.g. waterlogging/salinity in canal tracts and depletion of ground water resources in tube-well irrigated areas). They raise the question of sustainability of irrigation-based agriculture. "Under irrigated farming the problem of sustainability arises, *inter alia*, from (i) drainage to ground-water aquifers from the intrusion of saline and brackish waters unfit for irrigation, and (ii) development of waterlogging/salinity within canal command areas".[12] These aspects deserve serious considerations. Surely hydrological mapping of irrigated landscapes can help in crystallising the area specific issues which can be taken care of by sound water management for sustainable development of regional agriculture.

In industrial planning the geographic contribution is valuable in analysis of location and development of industries, of most suitable and cost effective sites for the location of future plants of different industries, delineation of industrial regions of different orders and indication of their suitability for establishing industrial complexes and industrial estates. Here the geographer can profitably utilise appropriate cartographic techniques for perspective industrial planning which must be supported by sound environmental-economic considerations.

The geographer who is primarily concerned with spatial inter-connections and spatial changes, can make a significant contribution to the planning of transport and communications by forecasting the potential traffic, changes in trade routes, logistics and transportation planning on national, regional and local levels including city transportation. Maps are certainly very useful tools for such planning exercises as transport network is one of the most basic infrastructural requirement for sustaining the socio-economic growth of a country or a region and links the major industrial and commercial centres with the intermeshed hierarchical order of settlements ranging from the metropolises to tiny rural hamlets. An integrated transport network is a prerequisite for sustainable development and must be restructured to meet the new challenges. For example, the National Highways have been serving as the primary arteries of the national road network system. But now they are unable to meet the increasing demands of traffic and commodity flows. That is why there is need for development of the Expressways by converting some National Highways like the Bombay-Pune Expressway and the Bombay-Vadodara Expressway and also by converting some of their critical sections from 2 lanes to 4/6 lanes. For such restructuring of the road network system diagnostic surveys and perspective planning are *sine quo non*, for which mapping exercises are very useful. In fact for such alignment surveys computerised mapping[13] holds great possibilities. Similarly, mapping of traffic flows and bottlenecks can help in replanning of the transport system of a metropolitan city like Delhi and making it more efficient for handling increasing demands. Perhaps the metro may provide an alternative strategy whereby the road traffic may be reduced and air and noise pollution may be controlled.

T.N. Khoshoo has aptly remarked :

> "The planners have to come up with developmental strategies which ensure sustainability of resource base. Implicit in it is the element of renewability. In simple words, the gains in productivity are managed in a manner which permit continuation of socio-economic development in the long run. Obviously planning for sustainable development has necessarily to be multi-disciplinary and trans-sectoral in character".[14] Cartography can contribute to these planning endeavours in a substantive manner.

## REFERENCES


1. Agarwal, Anil et al., (1992) : CSE Statement on Global Environmental Democracy, *Social Change*, Vol. 22(1), p.9.
2. *Ibid.*, p.10.
3. Young, Mike (1992) : Sustainable Investment : The Economic Challenge. *Environment and Development*, No. 166, UNESCO : Taylor and Francis, p. 113.

4. Charles, P. Kindleberger (1985) : *Economic Growth and Development*, V.K. Publishers : Ambala, p.3.
5. Planning Commission (1990) : Approach to the Eighth Five Year Plan 1990-95, p.65.
6. Mukherjee, Ramakrishna (1989) : *The Quality of Life : Valuation in Social Research*, Sage Publications : New Delhi.
7. Kunhen, F. (1992) : Sustainability, Regional Development and Marginal Locations, *Applied Geography and Development*, Vol. 39, p.101.
8. *Ibid.*, p.102.
9. Young, Mike (1992) : Sustainable Investment, *op. cit.*, fn.3, p.112.
10. Singh, L.R. (1972) : The Role of Applied Geography in National Planning in India, 21st International Geographical Congress : Selected Papers, Calcutta, p.180.
11. Pant, Pitamber (1962) : *Urbanization and Long Range Strategy, India's Urban Future*, Los Angeles, pp. 190-91.
12. Dhawan, B.D. (1989) : Water Resource Management in India : Issues and Dimensions, *Indian Jounal of Agricultural Economics*, Vol. 44(3), p.233.
13. Kantawala, H.B. (1992) : Computerised Highway Survey Mapping, XII INCA Conference, New Delhi.
14. Khoshoo, T.N. (1986) : Developmental Priorities in India and Sustainable Development, Indian Science Congress, New Delhi, p.5.

**FOURTH**

# ECOLOGICAL PERSPECTIVE OF ECONOMIC PLANNING IN U.P. HIMALAYAS

G.C. TEWARI

Despite four decades of planned developmental efforts by the State to alleviate the bite of adverse ecological conditions in the Himalayan districts of Uttar Pradesh, the intractable roots of frustration of the local population still relate to ecological degeneration and its linkages with unscientific exploitation of the region's natural resources.

Ecological security and economic justice to the hill man constitute the raw nurve of the local psyche. The protagonists of the Uttrakhand movement have built their case on these very issues. One may call this their frustration, nevertheless it is not something that can be dismissed lightly. For, left to itself, the fast accumulating frustration of the people can degenerate and lead this nascent mass movement on the lines similar to those of Gorkhaland, Jharkhand and the Bodo agitations.

The region to which this paper refers consists of the northern hill zone of Uttar Pradesh which is encompassed within the 'hill region', and constitutes 98 per cent of its total surface. And the questions the paper seeks to answer are as follows : In what overt forms do the ecological problems manifest inside the hill districts? What is the magnitude of the problem? How ecological degradation in the area is related to the economic management of its natural resources ? What are the basic features of the economic development model that is being implemented for the past four decades? And, lastly, how the economic development process in the area can be synchronized with the demands of ecological preservation of the region on the one hand, and an overall economic advancement of the native population, on the other?

The presentation is divided into three parts. Part-I highlights the tell-tale evidence of wide-spread ecological degradation inside the region. Critical appraisal of four decades of planning effort is presented in Part-II. And in Part-III an attempt has been made to sketch the outlines of an alternative paradigm of economic development which could combine economic development with eco-stability and distributional justice inside the region.

## I

## ECOLOGICAL DEVASTATION MAGNITUDE AND CONSEQUENCES

The tell-tale evidences of ecological destruction in the hill districts of U.P. are too many to be recounted in this paper. However, the aftermath of eco-instability touches the common man at several points in his day to day life. They range from an acute scarcity of fuel wood and fodder, spurt in the range and destructive power of unpredictable floods and landslides, growing signs of desertification over wide stretches of the landscape, to drying up of water holes, siltation of grass and bushes by road debris, and mounting rate of annual loss to life and property during and immediately after the rainy season.

Scarcity of fuel and fodder is forcing successive generations of fuelwood pikers to travel over longer distances, and spend more time in collecting a head load of fuelwood. In the twenty-four sample villages of Alakhnanda, Pinder and Bhagirathi rivers, in district Chamoli, the effective forest lines have receded from an average distance of 0.5 km to about 4 to 5 km within a period of three generations, and the average period of fuel collection of the villages has increased from 20 days a year to about 5 months a year. In some villages, nesting in the narrow gorge of mountain valleys, the women are travelling ten to fifteen kilometres a day to bring home a head-load of firewood for the hearth (Tewari, 1989).

Landslides in the hill districts have become an endemic phenomenon, and the enormous volume of the resulting sediment is filling the reservoirs, and chocking the streams. The Ichari Dam, on river Tons, was filled with sediments up to the level of the crust of the spillway, 160 meter high, within just two years, 1975 to 1977. The total sediment carried into the lake was of the order of 29 million cubic meters in 1978-79 (Valdiya, 1987). The rate of sedimentation behind the 12 meter high Kalagarh Dam, in Ramganga river, is so enormous that the projected life of the dam has been reduced from 185 years to 48 years (Valdiya, 1987).

Measurements on the satellite pictures show that the flood plains of the rivers and streams in this region, which cover nearly 5 per cent of the total area, is increasing steadily at an average rate of 5 to 10 per cent per year (Valdiya, 1987). Due to massive soil erosion, 40 to 50 per cent of natural springs in the area east of the Nainital town have either completely dried up or have turned seasonal (Valdiya, 1987). Of the 126 water holes that existed in the 24 villages in Alakhnanda, Pinder and Bhagirathi catchments some three to four decades ago, 35 have gone completely dry, and the remaining have become seasonal with considerable reduction in water discharge (Tewari, 1989).

A common feature of a desert country is the 'too little, too much water syndrome'. The region is fast approaching such a scenario. The difference in volume of water during the dry and rainy seasons in the rivers and rivulets has become abnormally high. Mounting evidences of extensive invasion by Xerophytic plants on the naked mountain slopes skirting river valleys, indicates that the process of desertification has already begun, and that the 'thermostat' of the ecological system is steadily giving way.

The restorative mechanism of eco-stability in the region is provided by the forests and the grass-lands. This is so because forests are the main force which shape the input-output mechanism of the energy-system in this region. Human interference with earth's surface, in whatever form, ultimately impinges on forest vegetation, and the thermostatic mechanism of the eco-system, which helps to moderate the extreme fluctuations in the functioning of the natural systems, also operates through the life cycle of forest regeneration.

In such a region where forests constitute the main life line of the eco-system, nearly 1,038,000 hectare of forest land today lies in highly degraded and defoliated condition. Known as civil soyam forests these areas, were lush and green forests only about a century ago, but today they are the main theatre of frequent land slides and constant soil erosion inside the region.

The crown density in the reserved forests, which constitute two-third of the reported forest area, is far from satisfactory. In Kumaon where 33 per cent of the surface area is covered with tree cover, barely 1.6 per cent of this can claim a canopy density of 60 per cent and above. According to the land imagery indications only 28.7 per cent of the Central Himalayan Sector is forested and of this only 4.4 per cent has a crown density more than 60 per cent.

The excessive rate of extraction of forest produce in the region has overstepped the carrying capacity of nature. In Kumaon Himalayas the grazing pressure is 2.5 to 4.25 times greater than the carrying capacity of the forests and the grass lands. Every year approximately 4.54 million cubic meter of wood is extracted from the forests of this region. If this high rate of extraction of forest produce which is 5.8 per cent per year is not reduced, the regeneration of these forests will cease completely by A.D. 2031 (Shah, 1981).

In Kumaon Himalayas, the incidence of grazing is 2.4 times the carrying capacity of the forests in Chamoli district, 4.5 times in Almora district and 2.4 times in Chakrata tehsil of Dehradun district (Singh and Sexena, 1978). At 5 per cent annual at which the grass lands in Kumaon are loosing their productivity they would also meet their nadir by A.D. 2041 (Shah, 1981).

The construction of roads has been one of the most devastating experience of the Himalayan eco-system. Starting from a scratch in 1960, the region today has a span of more than 44,000 km of metalled and dirt roads which often cut through cones of fossil land slide – debris, called screen-fans, and periodically activate them. The excavation of one kilometer stretch of road requires removal of 40,000 to 80,000 cubic meters of debris. Thus the construction of 44,000 km of roads generated about 2640 million cubic meters of debris which sliding down the slopes destroys vegetation, kills springs and clogs water coursing downslope (Valdiya, 1985). After the roads are constructed they are ravaged recurringly during rains by landslides and rockfalls.

The pattern of landuse is one of the most persistent enemy of eco-stability. Here 63 per cent of the population lives in 9.7 per cent land area and the cultivation is confined to river valleys of extremely restricted area, or the gentler slopes in lower altitudes (Valdiya, 1987). The pressure on land, 17.6 persons per hectare of cultivable land, is excessive. The corresponding figures for U.P. plains are 2.0 to 5.8 persons per acre (Modie, 1981). The pressure is driving the people up the slopes, leading to encroachment of forests. In the last two decades the agricultural land has expanded by 58 per cent and 51 per cent respectively in the districts of Tehri and Uttar Kashi (R.K. Gupta, 1977), all at the cost of forests. As a result of such expansion of grain and millet cultivation about 25 per cent of the cultivated land in this area exists on unstable mountain slopes of 50° and more.

## II

## ECONOMIC DEVELOPMENT PHILOSOPHY AND ITS CONSEQUENCES

In the wake of planned development a new process of socio-economic change was introduced by gearing the economy of the region to market forces. In order to marginalise the place of millets and to arrest the process of reckless expansion of cultivated land along rainfed mountain slopes, efforts were made to introduce cash crops like soyabean; sunflower; fruits and potatoes.

The subsistence economy lacked an industrial sector. To remove this deficiency a set of manufacturing factories, based on the natural and human resources of the region, were commenced. And to facilitate unhampered growth of the commodity producing sector an elaborate infrastructure of power and transport was built.

The most important natural and human resources on which the new economic development process in the region could be based were the land and the mineral deposits; the forests and their annual produce; the scenic beauty of the landscape, low temperature, and dust free atmosphere throughout the year; and a fairly high rate of female literacy among young working women and their traditional work culture. However, the new development process selected only the land, the minerals and the forests for its use and completely overlooked the productive potential of the other factors.

Its economic philosophy placed its blind faith on the profit motive of the traders in the national markets to act as the main spring of economic development in the region and overlooked the interests of the native growers, producers and workers who, being small and unorganized economic units, were incapable of standing on their own against the rapacious interests of the organised and well entrenched trading houses in the Darwinian world of the so-called free market.

In the new paradigm of economic development, which unfolded in the wake of the planning era, the present-worth of a crop or mineral in the market, rather than the requirements of sustained and ecologically tenable and holistic development of the region's economy, became the raison d'etre for its exploitation as a productive resource.

The effort failed miserably as even after four decades of sustained endeavour the new economic process could not change the subsistence character of the region's economy. In agriculture millets and food grain cultivation for self consumption continued to predominate, and overshadow all efforts to raise commercial crops, while the march of the hoe, to break ever new grounds on progressively increasing gradients across the undulating surfaces of mountain slopes to raise marginal crops, continued merely as ever.

In an identical fashion the industrial process also failed to make even a slightest dent on the poverty and unemployment of the native population.

The opening up of the region to unbridled market forces reinforced the 'back wash effect' of economic development that occurred elsewhere in the State and the country. The new exchange relationship that developed between the area and the wider economy through market forces, failed to create economic motivation where it was needed most. Its sole purpose was to exploit mineral, forest, human, and other primary resources to support the accelerating process of economic development elsewhere in the country. Within the region the little development that took place, largely as a by-product, remained strictly couched within the exploitative paradigm of a colonial economy which existed not for its own benefit but for providing primary sustenance to the mother economy, which in this case was the national economy, outside this region.

Some glimpses of how the agricultural and the industrial economy of the hill districts fared under the new dispensation of growth and development can be seen in the following scenario.

Madwa is a course millet. It is consumed by the poorest among the village people. In 1985-86, after 34 years of planned development efforts, the acreage under this kharif crop covered an area which was larger than that of rice in four hill districts of Garhwal Mandal, and almost equal to rice acreage in Almora and Pithoragarh districts of Kumaon. The innovative crop Soyabean covered an area which was barely 0.22 per cent of the acreage under Madwa in the Garhwal Mandal, and 0.18 per cent in Kumaon. Fruit cultivation, for which ideal agro-climatic conditions existed occupied an area which was barely 1.6 per cent of the coverage under Madwa in Kumaon, and 0.14 per cent in Garhwal.

Cultivation of sunflower (oil) seeds was non-existent in Garhwal Mandal and hardly noticeable in Kumaon.

Potato, the most favoured cash crop of the region, was being cultivated over an area which was 5.5 per cent of the area under the millet crop in Kumaon, and 5.7 per cent in Garhwal Mandal.

Though agriculture is the main source of livelihood for over 90 per cent of rural households, yet less than two per cent of the production of major crops – wheat, paddy and Madwa – is marketed, and the proportion of households reporting for sale was not even one per cent of cultivating households (Joshi, B.K. 1987).

In the case of most of the households agricultural produce could at best meet a few months requirements of food grains, for the rest they had to depend on the purchases from the market.

Roads and other means of transport have only strengthened the process of outward migration of able bodied persons in search of livelihood. The incidence of migration for outside jobs among men was found to be higher in villages connected with motorable roads then others (Joshi, B.K., 1987). And the excessive pressure of population on cultivable land – 17.6 persons per hectare – is driving people up the mountain slopes leading to encroachment of forest lands.

The attempt to give a manufacturing arm to the region's economy turned out equally frustrating. The industrial sector of the 'Hill Region' in 1980-81 consisted of 185 manufacturing units, of which 23 per cent of the installed and 24 per cent of the licensed capacity, lay unutilised.

From the stand point of agro-climatic conditions and the level of economic development, the 'Hill-Region' of Uttar Pradesh is sharply divided into two parts. Four-Fifth of it, which is mountaineous and economically backward, consists of six full and two half districts. The districts of Nainital and Dehra Dun, encompass large areas of the Gangetic Plains within their boundaries.

In 1981-82, 83 per cent of the industrial capacity and 93 per cent of industrial output of the region was cornered by these developed narrow strips of Tarai and Doons. Industrial employment, likewise, remained concentrated in these parts. In 1981, as against the average daily employment of 20,377 industrial workers in Nainital and Dehradun districts, the per day average employment in the rest of the region's territory, comprising 6 districts, was barely 1623 workers. The rate of output return on invested capital for the Hill Region as whole was 29.66 per cent; it was 0.72 per cent above the average in the plains areas and 8.94 per cent below the average in the hilly tract.

Industrialization is an ever widening and constantly unfolding process of chain reaction between creation of additional capacity and generation of additional output. The former creates the latter which, in turn, induces creation of additional industrial capacity and so on goes the process in successive ripples gathering speed from its own momentum. The process of industrialisation unfolds itself through forward and backward linkages. Such a chain reaction process was never created, with the result that for the four-fifth part of the region, which is mountaineous, the positive impact of modern industries ever remained literally invisible, not more than one time thud (Tewari, 1987).

The negative impacts of the industrialisation process – that reduce the development potential by causing serious injury to the natural eco-systems are too numerous to be counted here. The most notorious in this regard are the ore-mining units. Their singular aim has been to dig out industrial ore-magnesite, talcum stone and calcium phosphate — and export these in crude raw material form, without an iota of value added through intermediate processing, to areas outside the region. The magnesite factories at Almora and Pithoragarh, the largest industrial units in this area, are engaged in mining operation for over three decades, during which they have done nothing except digging out the ore with wanton unconcern for the ecological stability of the region and exporting it in the most unprocessed form. There has been not a single attempt to diversify the production or to encourage ancillaries within their production line.

The pillage to earth surface, wrought by the hunters of calcium-phosphate ore near Mussorie, the reckless devastation caused by the traders of talcum stone in Pithorgarh district, the devastating air and water pollution, and structural instability caused by the dynamite blasts in the magnesite ore zones in Almora and Pithoragarh, are some of the examples of how the so called industrialisation process operates in this area.

The main reasons why the post-independence process of economic development could not change the basic character of the region's economy are as follows:

> *One*: the market mechanism, to which the infant economy was allied failed to develop the necessary backward linkages and create new production sectors. Nor did it ever make any conscious effort to revitalise the native sources of strength that existed, in whatever form or areas, in the traditional order. Thus it is pathetic to see that in a region for which wood and timber are the major items of export, even the minimum necessary facility for seasoning of the wood was not created. Or where the cultivation of potato as a cash crop was promoted at so heavy a cost, there is not even a single cold-storage facility available to store the local produce to protect the growers from the exploitative, tentacles of the distress sale phenomenon. The efforts to introduce cash crops failed not because they lacked profitable markets, or that production possibilities in the form of proper agro-

climatic conditions did not obtain. They failed solely because the new exchange process of the national market did not pay attention to the interests of the small and unorganised growers and manufacturers who had neither the backing of the collective bargaining organisations nor individual capacity to stay in the open market on their own.

*Two:* The planners of the developmental process failed to realise the infirmity of the surface bound resources as the basis of production, and could not foresee the disastrous consequences of large scale tempering with the earth surface in a geologically sensitive area.

*Third:* The planning process also erred in identifying the main springs of economic activity in this region. Opting to tread on the familiar path of economic development, its weakness lay in not being able to comprehend the enormous untapped potential that lay open in the productive use of the thermal and other unique properties of the climate. The dust-free atmosphere, and low atmospheric temperatures are bounties of nature which can scarcely be created artificially in laboratories, and which are the necessary conditions for electronic and other precision instrument manufacture.

It also overlooked the unbounded energy potential which can be tapped by building mini-dams across the mountain slopes and thousands of seasonal streams and gorges.

*Fourth:* It also failed to comprehend the basic character of the labour force of the region. Here the main economic agent for the major sectors of the economy is woman and not man. Thus, starting with the familiar sex bias in economic planning the leaders of the new development process failed to appreciate the productive potential of the female work-force; their proven ability to put up with hard work, and capacity to adapt to new lines of production.

*Lastly:* It failed to appreciate the most important fact that while on the surface the scope for all kind of economic activities may appear large, rational economic development in the region can be conducted along very narrow corridors only.

Thus, starting with a false step, the new economic development process went on creating mutually contradictory development schemes which only accelerated the process of ecological degradation. This not only made the task of monitoring of the degrading ecological scene difficult, and the steps to check the process disjointed and fitful, but also turned the entire development process itself into a totally sterile and an exercise in utter futility.

## Towards Eco-Development Planning

Social and economic planning in the outer Himalayan ranges area is a highly complex and difficult exercise. This is so because perhaps no where else in the country ecological considerations play such a vital role in prohibiting certain type of economic pursuits as they do in this region. Formulation of any action plan, which entails interference which the ecological systems of the region, even within narrow ranges, entails a virtual tight rope walking. Eco-suitability considerations not only severely narrow down the scope of agriculture and industry in their traditional form, but also ruthlessly dictate that the form and texture of the entire commodity producing sector should be defined within the narrow bounds set by them.

Eco-development considerations demand that social planning be based on ecological facts. But what are ecological facts? Ecological facts are defined through and continued by the ecological conception of the reality; by our realisation that all things are connected and interdependent, contributing to the total meaning of the habitat. Simply stated, we recognise that in addition to bricks and mortar, build environments provide spaces which are distinctly human; are impregnated with values and social cohesion which are distinctly human. The sum total of these trans-physical characteristics is the living history of a place. The human experience of the living history of a place is as much a fact as bricks and walls of a building.

The reason which recognises the importance of human ecology; which recognizes that places are rooted in living history as well as impregnated with values, is an ecological reason. The reason goes hand in hand with the ecological vision of reality of which an intrinsic aspect is the recognition of ecological facts. The opposite of this is a mechanistic reason. The exercise in economic planning in this region so far has been a mere pursuit of objective reason, attempting to rationalise the complex, subtle, multi-layered texture of social and human lives in the name of functionality and mechanical efficiency (so often conceived in the broad national framework of profit maximisation based on a hypothetical matrix of prices and costs), and that it was a colossal blunder. That while economising within the narrow frame of reference, we have issued to ourselves an enormous bill, as price for the developmental gains which, could at best be termed as sub-marginal.

Further, it needs to be appreciated that the ultimate objective of economic planning is not a mere satisfaction of material needs but to add to our stature as human beings. The modern concept of development is not mere economic affluence but improvement in the quality of life. Quality of life is hard to define, although its absence is readily apparent. There are, of course, a number of objective criteria – biological, economic and social – by which to judge the quality of life. Although some objective requirements must be fulfilled on the biological level as the first order condition, far more important for the attainment of the quality of life are existential prerequisites; the inner feeling of worth as a human being, the sense of dignity; the sense of anchor and belonging; the feeling of one's place in the world. All these existential attributes of quality of life, by and large, are generated by culture and religion in its philosophical manifestation.

The moral that flows from the above discussion on quality of life in the context of economic planning instrumentalities in this region, is that while the immediate priority for the region should be to create the necessary artifacts of the economic criteria, sufficient care needs to be taken to ensure that the pattern of development and the consequent economic prosperity does not destroy the basis of the existential prerequisites, in the absence of which mere satisfaction of material needs may lead to a totally empty and meaningless life; a life deprived of quality.

The conventional wisdom having failed to show results,

it is imperative that the current paradigm of economic development be replaced by a new plan capable of bringing the development process in the region in tune with the rhythm and direction of its genius; confine human interference with nature within nature's carrying capacity, and harmonise the economic activities with the existing and potential talents of its people.

The biggest hurdle in initiating such a process is the inertia of social action; the habit of treading on the beaten path, the fear of the uncommon and the unfamiliar. To break this hurdle we have not only to think big but also to act bold.

The do's and dont's which emanate from the structural peculiarities of the resource base of the region point to certain guidelines for minimising the social and cultural costs of economic development. The broad objectives of economic development may be stated as follows :

(i) to marginalise the place of agricultural production in the domestic product of the region;
(ii) to make industry as the main stay of livelihood for the native population;
(iii) to enable the marginal and unorganised cultivators and other producers of commodities of the region to identify their self interest in the rapid structural transformation of their subsistence economy. To achieve this, to create appropriate organisational and price incentives for them within the new market structure to which they have been tied; and
(iv) to make vigorous R & D efforts to discover such new possibilities of commodity production in the region which can be carried out without destabilising the ecological balance of the area.

Sectoral interpretation of these objectives implies that in the industrial sector the aim should be :

(a) to make optimum productive use of the unique thermal and dust-free qualities of the atmosphere. For this to develop the region as the main centre of production of electronic goods and precision industry products in the country, and to make effort that each village in the region develops into a viable centre of this decentralised production process;

(b) to assist the womenfolk of the region to emerge as the principal arm of the labour force working in these decentralised units of industrial production by making it possible for them to learn the skills of the new trades largely by doing and through on-the-job training. To assist this process, to open women – polytechniques and give service guarantee to their pass outs; and

(c) to stop the operations of such enterprises which need mining and deep digging of the earth till the time when new developments in technology make them a safe exercise from the point of view of ecological stability of the area.

It should be fully recognised that if the region does not diversify its economy into industrial sector it would even remain a country of such people who export their able bodied sons to serve as menials job hands in the eating houses and other low paid vocations of the informal sector in cities and towns outside this region, and import everything from food, fruits, foot-wears and even income through remittances.

Introduction of modern technology is essential for realising the full productive potential created by the bountiful nature in this region. But as important as is it, it is also true that high technology will never employ the number of people that our agriculture and the trading sector employs today. So the answer does not lie in promoting high technology at the expense of our basic vocations – family farming and horticulture, but to promote both of these together. In other words the region needs a rational economic development policy, the objectives of which in agriculture should be :

(a) to replace grain and millet cultivation by and large by cash crops farming and horticulture, and to explore the possibilities of promoting allied economic activities like honey farming and commercial cultivation of flowers, medicinal plants and herbs; and

(b) to wean out grain, millet and potato cultivation from the rain-fed terraces of mountain slopes having more than 30° of inclination.

The latest fad of the planners is the tourist industry.

With state assistance and subsidies gigantic efforts are at foot to develop a tourist industry of international standard in this region and to help it to become the main plank of the new economic development process.

The tourist potential in the region, of course, can not be totally overlooked. However, a word of caution about large scale promotion of tourism at the current stage of development of the region's economy, is in order. It is essential that any new scheme for social and economic development, like this, must be thoroughly evaluated for its likely consequence in the region before putting it on the ground.

Looked exclusively from the view point of commerce the region has considerable potential for the development of tourism. On a priori reasoning there is also a strong case in favour of adopting tourism as the main vehicle of economic growth and social development in this region which is severely deficient in industrial and agricultural production and is bereft of employment opportunities.

However, there are some other aspects which caution us against taking a hasty decision in this matter. Tourism would add to population pressure in the region. The pressure is caused both by the influx of tourists, and also by those who seek to provide them services or trade in the commodities of tourist demand. Tourism, being a service industry, would engross the entire region within its fold. Increased population would not remain confined to a few developed hill stations, instead it will invade all the nooks and corners of the region which are on the routes to places of tourist fancy.

Large scale development of tourism, which would increase the pressure of population in the region, would, therefore, augment the rate of depletion of the local forest, as "there is a strong functional relationship between the quantum of fuel wood collection from the forest and the size of village population in this region" (Tewari, 1989). The damage would further compound if the spurt in tourist demand also sets in a process of unauthorised construction of tourist houses, hotels, cafeterias and other tourist amenities, at structurally unstable sites.

A region benefits from the tourist trade because it creates a situation of abnormal profits in a sellers market for those who have their own products to sell. However, if the region is deficient in the production of such goods which are demanded by the tourists these will be imported, and in that event, the profits will go to the outsiders.

Prosperity of the common man through the development of tourism in a poor area is a myth. A region gains from tourist trade in real terms only when the tourist trade develops strong production linkages with the production sector of the local economy. The wage component of the tourist industry is always very small.

Looking at the current state of production of marketable goods in the region it is apparent that profitable economic linkages do not exist between tourism and the local economy. It is, therefore likely that the region will benefit from the high pitched demand for articles of consumption created by the tourist industry. Further, the impact of tourist demands in a region, which is deficient in commodity production, is often morally degrading. Those who have nothing else to sell in the market are often lured by the easy money in contraband trafficking and white slavery. Tourism, which flourishes on the high consumption propensity of the nova-riche, materialising in the form of high pitched, morally un-inhibited demand provides a fertile ground for the growth and expansion of a variety of anti social professions. One can not be totally blind to this aspect.

Government planning doesn't have to mean either socialism or anarchy. All it means is a game plan, an objective. It means coordinating all pieces of economic policy instead of setting them piece-meal. In the prevailing mood of development at any cost, the concept of long-term perspective has become a loaded term. The impatience of the official planners is really astounding, as they want to achieve everything immediately through a quick fix by companies and enterprises run by swashbucking entrepreneurs. The social realities are largely ignored, the moral issues avoided, and the current distribution of income and wealth is accepted as given, and unchangeable. Sustained development does not come this way. It needs a holistic view, patient planning and a good deal of managerial skill.

## REFERENCES

Drysek, John, S. (1987) : *Rational Ecology, Environment and Political Economy*, Basil Blakwell.

Gupta, R.K. (1977) : Watershed in the Right Approach to Ecosystem Management — Paper in Himalayan Mountain Ecosystems, Macmilan Bhawan, New Delhi.

Joshi, B.K. (1987) : Agriculture in the Economy of Uttarakhand; Preliminary Results — Study Based on a Study of Eight Village Clusters — Seminar Paper ; "Rain-fed Agriculture in the Himalayan Regions of India, Pant Nagar.

Menard, H.W. (1989) : Some Rates of Regional Erosion, *Journal of Geol.*

Moddie, A.D. (1981) : Himalayan Environment — Paper in The Himalayas, Ed. : J.S. Lal, Oxford University Press, New Delhi.

Shah, S.L. (1981) : Ecological Degradation and Future of Agriculture in Himalayas, Presidential Address, 41st All India Agricultural Economic Conference, Indian Society of Agricultural Economist, New Delhi.

Tewari, G.C. (1989) : Ecological and Economic Management of Forests in U.P. Himalayas, Mimeograph, G.B. Pant Social Science Institute, Allahabad.

Valdiya, K.S. (1985) : Accelerated Erosion and Landslide Prone Zones in the Himalayan Region. In : J.S. Singh (Edited) *Environmental Regeneration in Himalayas : Strategies and Concepts*, Central Himalayan Environmental Association, Nainital.

Valdiya, K.S. (1987) : *Environmental Geology — Indian Context*, McGraw Hill.

FIVE

# NEW PERSPECTIVES IN DEVELOPMENT ADMINISTRATION IN INDIA

K.B. SRIVASTAVA

## Introduction

At the dawn of Independence, rural India was characterised by abject poverty, illiteracy, ignorance and exploitation of poor by landlords and traders. The new task set out for the Government of Independent India was to work for human betterment, fulfilment, the enrichment of lives through exploitation of unexplored resources and equitable distribution of benefits. The stated task required multi-pronged approach to development and this could not obviously be carried out by the administrative machinery inherited from the colonial rule. Considering the magnitude of job and the environment in which this was to be pursued, it was rightly perceived that without joint efforts of the administration, elected representatives and rural people, the expected results could not be accomplished. The increase in scale, change in contents and the need to make the administration responsive and result oriented led to conceptualization of the administrative process involved in developmental activities as 'Development Administration'. The new administrative process was formally launched on second October, 1952. After four decades of sustained efforts of development administration it can be said now that their achievements were impressive in all the fields including agriculture, irrigation, dairy production and industries. Food production has increased from 55.0 m mt in 1950-51 to 170 m mt in 1989-90; total irrigation potential was expanded from 9.7 m ha in 1950-51 to 30.5 m ha in 1984-85 and nearly 50 m ha by the close of the 1990's; the share of agriculture in GDP had suitably declined from 56 per cent in 1951 to 38.2 per cent in 1984-85; dairy production has increased rapidly from 17 m mt at the dawn of independence to 52 m mt in 1990; once heavily dependent on dairy imports, India became self-sufficient in dairying by the turn of the 1980's.[1] After introduction of several development programmes, the poor people have begun to hope that their life will be better in the near future. Nevertheless, development administration continued to be criticised for non-performance on the ground that the results were not achieved as rapidly as expected and that it maintained its elite character, unhelpful attitude and inordinate delay in transacting governmental business. In the course of its evolution, several structural and operational changes were affected in the new administrative system with a view to streamline its functioning. In a fresh attempt to make the administration more responsive to the people, the Panchayati Raj Institutions (PRIs) are being strengthened so as to making them vibrant and to enabling them share responsibilities with the administration in the task of socio-economic transformation of India. In the changed perspective, it is felt necessary to examine the strength and weaknesses of development administration, and to suggest structural and operational reforms in the system for better performance.

## Changing Horizon of Development Administration

The development administration was conceived as a tool for alround balanced development of the country to ensure a rising national income and steady improvement in living standard of the people over a period of time. It was emphasised that the organization of services and resource allocation on an area basis, co-ordinated action for implementation of programmes and association of local organizations in advisory capacity would be ideal administrative strategies for achieving the goals set out for the nation. The Community Development (CD) Programme launched in 1952-53 through a comprehensive administrative structure created at a newly unit called Development Block was a major step towards area based approach and coordinated action for the development of rural areas. Later, establishment of the PRIs with the stated tasks of facilitating people's participation, empowering them (the people) and in the process making administration responsive to the people provided organizational support to the development administration. In the course of its operation, the development administration touched the lives of millions of people, gave them new hopes and aspirations, and thereby changed the face of rural India considerably. But sooner than later it was realised that our developmental energies created imbalances in the society and by early seventies it became common knowledge that the fruits of developmental efforts were reaped mostly by the rich and the affluent sections of the society while poor and landless gained, if at all, less.[2]

With a view to reducing disparities in the society, several special programmes for target groups were initiated and separate autonomous agencies created at the district level for their implementation. The creation of multiple agencies signified a change in administrative action from the hitherto coordinated efforts to sectoral (isolated) approach. As a result, the sectoral officers who together constituted a Team for coordinated action no longer remained a part of the Team. The modified approach, however, envisaged a loose coordination by providing for constitution of Advisory Councils for such programmes engaged in multi-sectoral activities. It was suggested that the Council would consist of sectoral officers of appropriate sectors, elected representatives, and be chaired by Head of the district administration. All the states followed the suit, introduced suggested changes in the administrative system and constituted the Advisory Councils for respective programmes. But as the things turned out, it was realised that the strategy of isolated efforts envisaged in sectoral approach could not achieve the desired results as the success of special programmes required multi-sectoral approach. The Advisory Councils failed to serve as an effective organ for coordinated action. There was, therefore, need to restructure the administration again so as to make it an effective vehicle for social change. The steps taken to revitalise the PRIs and introducing decentralised planning and implementation system are the steps in this direction. After adopting the decentralised planning and implementation process with the district as its operational unit the development administration has been made responsible not only for implementation of the plan proposals but also for preparation of the plan. The decentralised district planning followed by devolution of financial powers to the district planning body, and bestowing on the PRIs the responsibilities relating to implementation of the plan proposals with emphasis on distributive justice have widened the scope of development administration and have, thus, opened new vistas in the areas of the development management.

*Challenge of Change*

The new decentralised system has thrown new challenges before the administration in several ways. While performing the tasks relating to planning, the administration has to ensure that the district plan not only supplements the efforts of national and state plans but also tries to fill the gaps which remained uncovered in the process of planned development with due priority to local needs and aspiration of the people. The new dispension requires administration a good deal of consultations with the rural masses and elites and effective harnessing of traditional expertise of local communities. As an implementor, the administrator has to ensure that the programmes are implemented not only in their spirit but also accommodate the directions given by the elected representatives. But the data from field, collected at the initial stage, reveal that the sailing has not been smooth for the administration. It would, therefore, be pertinent to look at the constraints the development administration have been facing in performing their new mandate.

## Administration of Decentralised Planning

In the absence of comprehensive planning machinery at the district level, the plans are prepared by different sectoral officers in the districts. While doing, so, they (the sectoral officers) are required to : (1) adhere to the `guidelines' issued by the State Government and to keep in mind the funds available for different sectors in the districts; and (2) consult the local people so as to ensure that the plans reflect people's felt needs and aspirations. Under these conditions, it often becomes difficult for a sectoral planner to do justice with his sector. It has been reported that quite often the money allocated for a particular sector is just sufficient to complete the ongoing projects and thus leaves no scope for proposing new projects. Even if some new projects are formulated and included in the district plan initially, sometimes they are dropped on the pretext that the projects do not fall with in the priority areas. With regard to consultation it has been observed that in some places, the planners consult the representatives of various interest groups. As the system is new, we do not have nation-wide data to show the extent to which the process of consultations have been real in different states. However, our own study conducted recently in Maharashtra state revealed thus : "... the sectoral planners have not yet been able to evolve a suitable method for consultation with the people or their representatives and as a result the sectoral plans always did not include such subjects considered as priority areas of the local people"[3] The moot point is what would be the ideal device for consultation with the people? Going by the findings of our study referred to above, "... an ideal device for facilitating consultation with the people in planning process would be discussions of plan proposals in the Gram Sabha meetings."[4] This method indeed involves onerous responsibilities on sectoral planners, for, they can no longer depend on 'traditional' method of preparing plan on the basis of 'documented' information.

**Implementation of Plan Proposals**

It has been concluded by several studies that with the increase in their awareness and desire for better living, the people have started participating at various stages of planning and implementation of development programmes. Consequently their expectations from administration (government) have increased manifolds. In the prevailing situation, it is becoming day-by-day difficult for the administration to come nearer to the expectations of the people. The reasons for this state of affairs are several folds. Some of them are; (i) resource crunch; (ii) weak local organisations; (iii) limited autonomy; and (iv) shortage of technical staff.

(i) *Resource Crunch*

The experience of implementing government aided programmes so far suggests that these programmes could not build up local capacity but conversely increased the dependence and expectations of the people from the government. As at present the people expect considerable financial support from government in the development activities. This is more pronounced in the case of rural poor. But the Government with limited resources could not support all developmental programmes. Hence, there is a need that people should also contribute in either cash or kind or both. This will help in two ways : (i) a resource commitment will make the contributors more concerned for the success of development programmes, and (ii) the attitudes of development personnel will undergo change when they find that the people are making contributions. Cermea writes : In fact, the official requirement that local communities contribute a fraction of investment costs turns out to affect not only communities but the technicians' behaviour as well; it makes the planners and engineers more concerned with consulting the peasants than before, with getting the peasants' assent and contribution, and with actually involving them in the works.[5] In our given situation it is argued that rural people, by and large, are poor and are not capable to make resource commitment. But going by the experience gained at the initial stage of community development programmes when people contributed in cash or kind enthusiastically, there is no reason to believe that this could not happen at the present juncture. Hence, there is a need to reduce the dependence of the people on the governmental support and to encourage them to make resource commitment. These steps will benefit in two ways : (i) supplement the governmental efforts in a considerable way; and (ii) ensure real participation of the people in the developmental process. In the coming days the administration will have to direct their energies to achieving the above goals.

(ii) *Weak Local Organisations*

It has not been possible for the field administration to reach every individual. They ascertain the problems and expectations of the people through local organisations. Local organisations of the poor do not exist everywhere. The PRIs wherever existing serve this purpose to a limited extent. In the non-PRIs areas it is left at the administration to perform this job the way he deemed fit. Initially it was expected that the PRIs would be able to serve as a most desirable instrument for ascertaining the expectations of the people but later it was noted that due to several inherent shortcomings in them, they remained, by and large, ineffective. In the absence of any effective link between the people and the administration, it became difficult for the administration to ascertain the problems and needs of the people and thus they could not meet their expectations. After the passage of 73rd Constitution Amendment Bill, it is hoped that the PRIs will acquire a better image and will receive support of all sections of the people. In the emerging scenario, it is expected that the administration will utilise these institutions as a means to meet the expectations of the people and provide them (the rural people) meaningful support in raising their socio-economic status.

(iii) *Limited Autonomy*

The administrative decentralisation requires a real delegation of powers so as to allow enough autonomy to enable each sub-unit (below the State) to adjust to its special needs. After adopting the policy of administrative decentralisation steps have been taken to provide operational and financial autonomy to district administration. But in reality they enjoy only limited autonomy as their decision-making powers are limited to : prioritisation of schemes, decision on location of projects and suggestion with regard to appropriation of budgetary allocations. It may be further added that even there decision-making powers are not absolute because the administration at any given level are required to act in harmony with elected representatives of democratic structure (PRIs) existing at that level. It has been reported, time and again, that there were difference of opinion between the administration and the elected representatives on the matters relating to location of projects, distribution of benefits, etc. The ideal way of taking decisions on these aspects are to take into account the locational advantages and disadvantages and prospective beneficiaries of the projects in terms of distributive justice. This, notwithstanding, the administration has to accept the realities of democratic polity and to shape their functioning in such ways as to subserve the cause of building rural India.

(iv) *Shortage of Technical Staff*

After introduction of special programmes, the work load of the administrative machinery at the Block level has increased several fold. As usual, whenever a new programme is launched necessary administrative infrastructure in the form of autonomous bodies/agencies is created or relevant department is provided with technical support at the district level but only sporadic efforts are made to strengthen the technical component of the Block administrative machinery who actually implement the programmes. Taking their present work load into account, the Block machinery is required to help in the implementation of special programmes like Integrated Rural Development Programmes (IRDP), Jawahar Rozgar Yojna (JRY), Jal Dhara, etc., besides carrying out their traditional functions of planning and implementation of sectoral programmes, In the circumstances, it has become difficult for the administration at the cutting edge level (Block level) to do justice with new programmes. Hence, there is a need to strengthen the block administration by providing technical support commensurate to their work load.

**Responsive Bureaucracy**

In the beginning of post-independence era the Indian bureaucracy was criticised on the ground that it has imbibed the authoritarian and paternalistic attitude towards the masses, and that its structural characteristic was considered unsuited for a free India.[6] The implicit assumption was that the bureaucracy if charged with the responsibility of implementing development programmes would be serving only as an instrument of the vested interests. The Community Development Programme (CDP) followed by the establishment of Panchayati Raj bodies were conceived in the hopes that the bureaucracy will change their attitude and behaviour so as to carry out the developmental objectives of the country and to attune the people to avail of the opportunities available to them through plans and schemes of the government. But these initiatives could not bring out required changes in the functioning of deve-lopment bureaucracy and, thus failed to achieve its broader objectives.

Reporting in 1967 about the shortcomings of district administration, the Administrative Reforms Commission (ARC) listed among others the following main grievances of the people[7] :

(i) Unhelpful attitude of officials;
(ii) Inordinate delay in transacting government business; and
(iii) Unsatisfactory progress of Community Development Programmes.

One of the major constraints in improving the performance of district administration, as perceived by the ARC, was concentration of powers in the hands of bureaucracy. This was true during the initial years of community development because there was no effective people's organisation existing at the grass root level which could be entrusted upon even a part of responsibilities relating to implementation of development programmes. As a result more and more responsibilities and powers concerning implementation of development programmes were thrust upon the development bureaucracy. But there should be some limits to what bureaucracy could do. Nirmal Mukarji aptly points out : "Beyond a point expanding the bureaucracy or enhancing its powers and functions begins yielding reduced returns, and a stage comes when the benefits actually became negative."[8] In fact before ARC submitted its report, the State Government had already affected structural changes in the functioning of bureaucracy at district and below level by introducing Panchayati Raj system with a view to sharing the responsibilities of the bureaucracy. But the Panchayati Raj Institutions (PRIs) could not prove to be the effective instruments. In fact when the Panchayati Raj bodies were constituted, it was dimly perceived that the bureaucracy had its limits and the masses were gradually becoming awakened. The report of the ARC set the trends for introducing reforms in the administration at the district and below level. Measures like strengthening of the PRIs, evolving scheme of distribution of powers through relevant Acts between the bureaucracy and the office-bearers of the PRIs, providing autonomy to the district administration so as to act promptly for redressal of grievances, decentralising planning and implementation process with due emphasis on exploitation of local resources and fulfilment of people's aspirations, etc. were taken. But inspite of the fact that the efforts were made to make the bureaucracy share power with the elected representatives of the Panchayati Raj bodies, it was noticed that there struggle for power in the reformed system and that the influence the elected representatives exercised on the decision-making caused strains on the administration. In the given situation, it became a difficult task to strike a balance between one set up of forces and the other. But with the changing needs and demands of the time it appears that the bureaucracy despite the greed for power has realised that they have to work within the norms of democratic system.

At present, it is reported that they have accepted the supremacy of the elected representatives and have been giving due attention to the advice and suggestions rendered by them. It is heartening to note that wherever these institutions (PRIs) worked in harmony with the administration (or *vice-versa*) and implemented development projects in unison, it has shown good results. For instance, after primary education was transferred to the Panchayat Samitis in Rajasthan, it was found that there was marked improvement in enrollment of children in the schools and the teachers were found more regular in attending to the teaching work, and there was improvement in the standard of education. In West Bengal, the implementation of National Rural Employment Programme (NREP) by Gram Panchayats registered phenomenal success. In other states also, it has been noted with satisfaction that wherever PRIs were associated with the implementation and monitoring of development projects it resulted in greater success with regard to speed and economy. Their association ensured proper selection of beneficiaries, right location of projects, and participation of the people. On the contrary, there are sufficient indications to show that the development projects that were implemented by the official machinery without the support and help of the PRIs were treated like casual programmes and thus did not yield the desired results.

The recent studies covering various facets of Indian administration[9] have reported that there have been a marked improvement in the attitude and behaviour of bureaucracy over the earlier administrative machinery designed to handle only law and order and revenue collection matters. Our own study found that "... the bureaucracy (Development Administration) has realised that it cannot understand the problems of the beneficiaries (rural poor) or cannot wipe out the smugness and complacency in them without patronising them. There has been perceptible changes in the attitude of bureaucracy and its responsiveness to the people has also increased."[10] The study further reported that, "however the pace of change has been sluggish and slow".[11] There must have been genuine difficulties before the bureaucracy in performing the assigned tasks rapidly. This needs to be explored properly.

**Dysfunctional Tendencies**

By way of looking at some of the problems which largely hinder the effective performance of the bureaucracy. Several scholars have analysed the bureaucratic phenomenon from different angles. In one way or the other they are in agreement with the fact that bureaucracy in general is subject to many dysfunctions such as impersonality, slowness, the tendency to mistake organizational conventions for ultimate goals, etc.[12] In our system such dysfunctions have become established norms. Writing as late as in 1985, Dwivedi and Jain reported that the bureaucracy in India has followed the Weberian spirit of hierarchy so rigidly that mutual trust does not exist, either in inter-organizational relations or interpersonal relations in administration. "Mutual suspicion" is its prime tenet, leading to authorita-rianism among superiors, which destroy any team spirit with in the organisation. They further said that the bureaucracy in India, when confronted with a difficult decision, seldom makes any attempt to tackle the problem with initiative and imagination, but instead passes the problem to another department or makes a series of unnecessary references to subordinate to gain time.[13] But a development bureaucracy can ill-afford a strict adherence to the regulatory hierarchy where the main task of the administration is of encouraging innovation, initiative and identification with national objectives in every agency and official. A close observer of Indian administration would find that the dysfunction tendency of the bureaucracy, more particularly development administration segment, is on decline. Now they have started accepting the new challenges arising out of developmental actions. And with the process of decentralisation gathering momentum, the bureaucracy has got tremendous opportunities for new initiatives so as to get accelerated development. However, inspite of these opportunities the expected speed has not been coming forth in them. It may be because of their security of the service assured under the constitution or because non-performance has never been a ground for disciplinary action.

**Emerging Scenario**

The decentralised system of planning and implementation has been accepted as a major tool for achieving the developmental objectives set-forth by the Planning Commission. The Draft Eight Five Year Plan (1992-97) emphasised the need for building-up and strengthening of the institutions with which people are directly involved. It stated that the small community and village level institutions could be regarded as the cellular institutions, of which the entire body of the nation is built. Accordingly, the Eighth Plan has laid greater emphasis on institution building for rural development. It has envisaged that people's initiative and participation should be made key element in the process of development. The role of government should be to facilitate the process of people's involvement in developmental activities by creating the right type of institutional infrastructure particularly in rural areas. If the present indication is any guide to the future, the decentralisation process which has been set in is likely to be accelerated by changing the total complexion of the planning at the sub-state (District) level so that the major tasks of decision-making, project formulation and implementation are handled by the people through the democratic institutions and the state government shall provide them with the necessary back-up. The decentralised system has shown that it can yield better results if the planning process is fool-proof and implementation is effective with an inbuilt system of monitoring and evaluation in it.

A good plan cannot bring about desired results unless it

is followed by effective implementation. Rightly thus along with improving planning methodology, steps have been taken to transform the implementation set-up. For instance, the constitution of District Planning Boards has provided an opportunity for officials and non-officials to sit together and discuss the priority areas of the district plan. The move to strengthen the PRIs and thereafter to put the entire developmental machinery under the umbrella of Zilla Parishad will take the administration further nearer to the people. The development bureaucracy which in the beginning viewed development as its exclusive preserve and considered interference of elected representatives a hindrance to the speed and quality of development, is bound to change further its attitude and behaviour in the emerging set-up. In fact the bureaucracy has started realising that the democratically elected institutions at the local level (the PRIs) could be used favourably for the success of development projects. However, only a change in attitude and behaviour of bureaucracy will not make the system efficient, it is to be supplemented by sound procedures and practices, For instance, the relationship between officials and non-officials in the PRIs has to undergo a qualitative change. As at present both the segments (officials and non-officials) view the developmental issues from their own angles. If there is similarity in their view-points, it will help achieving the developmental objectives; but in the case of difference of opinions there will be a 'tug of war' between them which would adversely affect the achievement of results. Their relationship cannot be governed by the rules and regulations only. Suitable conventions in this regard are to be developed so that they do not detract from the broader objectives of development management.

The contributions of the erstwhile PRIs in the overall development of rural India cannot be undermined. It may be re-emphasised that wherever their continuity was maintained, the PRIs contributed immensely towards bringing a new social order in rural India. These institutions have also proved to be an effective instrument in filling the vacuum between the people and the bureaucracy. That said, these institutions have not been given fair trial by several states on one pretext or the other. In the context of decentralised administration, the state governments besides reconstituting the PRIs, should also strengthen the administrative infrastructure more particularly at the Block level in terms of adequate personnel with necessary expertise in planning and implementation of development programmes. Unless this is done the administration at the cutting-edge level cannot rapidly address itself to fulfilling the people's needs and aspirations.

## NOTES AND REFERENCES

1. Kurien, V. et al. (1992) : "Agriculture and Rural Development in the 1990's and Beyon : Redesigning the Chemistry between State and Institutions of Development", *Journal of Rural Development*, Vol. 11, No. 4, pp. 395-395.
2. The studies conducted by UNRISD and ILO corroborated the fact that increases in agricultural production benefited mostly the rich, specifically the landlords, the merchants and the owners of tractors and tube-wells, while the poor and landless gained less or did not gain or lost. As a result, the gap between the rich and the poor increased. See. for details :

   (a) UNRISD (1974) : *The Social and Economic Implications of Large Scale Introduction of New Varieties of Foodgrains*, Geneva, United Nations Research Institute for Social Development.

   (b) ILO (1977) : *Poverty and Landlessness in Rural Asia*, Geneva, International Labour Office.

3. Srivastava, K.B. (1991) : *Impact of Decentralisation on Rural Poor*, Hyderabad, National Institute of Rural Development (mimeo), pp. 90-91.
4. *Ibid.*, p. 91.
5. Cermea Michael M. (1983) : *A Social Methodology for Community Participation in Local Investments : The Experience of Mexico's PIDER Programme*, Washington D.C. The World Bank (Staff Working Paper No. 598), p. 4, Cf. Hari Mohan Mathur (1986) : *Administering Development in the Third World : Constraints and Choices*, New Delhi, Sage, p. 37.
6. Gaikwad, V.R. (1979) : "Bureaucracy at the District Level" In : S.C. Dube (ed.) *Public Services and Social Responsibility*, New Delhi, p. 15.
7. Government of India (1967) : Administrative Reforms Commission, Report of the Study Team on District Administration, New Delhi, p. 15.
8. Mukarji, Nirmal (1987) : "Some Issues in Decentralised Administration", In : Ramachandran Padma and Oomen, M.A. (eds.) *Some Issues in Development Administration*, New Delhi, Oxford & IBH, p. 27.
9. See, for instance, Mukarji, Nirmal (1987) : "Some Issues in Decentralised Administration" In : Ramachandran Padma and

Oomen, M.A. (eds.) *op. cit.*, and Ishwar Dayal : Challenges of Change in Government" In : S.C. Dubey (ed.) *op. cit.*

10. Srivastava, K.B. *op. cit.*, p. 108.
11. *Ibid.*, p. 109.
12. Chaturvedi, H.R. (1977) : *Bureaucracy and Local Community : Dynamics of Rural Development*, Bombay, Allied.
13. Dwivedi, O.P. and R.B. Jain (1985) : *India's Administrative State*, New Delhi, Gitanjali.

SIX

# DECENTRALISATION, DEVELOPMENT AND PANCHAYATI RAJ

SURESH MISHRA

Decentralised planning can be defined as planning at 'different levels' or a 'multi-level planning'. This may consist of planning at national level, state level, district level, block level or the village level or could be planning for a region. In other words decentralised planning is a system through which planning is attempted at different administrative and executive levels so that there is greater interaction between the developmental need and priorities of smaller areas (Micro regions) and different social classes with the sub-national and national levels, development policies and goals. Decentralised planning is neither a substitute to centralised planning nor an exclusive bottom-up process of planning. It is in fact a two way process which begins both at the top level (national and macro level) as well as at the bottom-level (local level) and merges with each other at a point below which centralised planning becomes irrelevant and above which micro-planning becomes meaningless.[1]

The objective of this paper is to examine the scope and effectiveness of decentralisation of planning and administration. The paper assumes that decentralisation can be conducive to more effective coordination and consistency, greater access to governmental services, increased involvement of the people in development planning, more effective delivery of public services for meeting basic human needs and increased accountability of governmental agencies.

## Need for Decentralisation

The growing interest in decentralised planning and administration is attributable not only to the disillusionment with the results of central planning and the shift of emphasis to growth-with-equity policies but also to the realisation that development is a complex and uncertain process that cannot be easily planned and controlled from the centre. Decentralisation is often justified as a way of managing national economic development more effectively and efficiently. But it is obvious that governments that have tried to decentralise during the 1950's, and 1960's have not always had effectiveness and efficiency as their primary goals. They have rarely embarked on a course of decentralisation primarily for economic reasons. Indeed, the economic impacts of decentralisation have not usually been calculated before hand. Thus recent experiments with decentralisation cannot be assessed entirely by economic criteria.

In many countries decentralisation is pursued in reaction to technical failure of comprehensive national development planning or the weak impact of multi-sectoral, macro-economic development programming. Neither of these have significantly increased the ability of Central Government to formulate, articulate and implement national development policies.[2]

**Objectives of Decentralisation**

Decentralisation is often seen as a way of increasing the ability of Central Government officials (bureaucracy) to obtain better and less suspect information about local and regional conditions, to plan local policies more responsively, and to react more quickly to unanticipated problems that inevitably arise during implementation.[3] In theory decentralisation should allow projects to be completed sooner by giving local managers greater discretion in decision-making so as to enable them to cut through the 'red tape' and the ponderous procedures often associated with the over-centralised administration.[4]

In some countries decentralisation is seen as a way of mobilising support for national development policies by making them better known at the local level. Local governments or administrative units, it is assumed, can be effective channels of communication between the national government and local communities. Greater participation in development planning and management supposedly promotes national unity by giving people, in different regions in a country, a greater ability to participate in planning and decision-making and thus increases their share in maintaining political stability. Greater equity in the allocation of resources for investment is presumed more likely when representatives of the weaker sections of the society participate in development decision-making.[5]

Moreover, decentralisation is an ideological principle associated with objectives of self-reliance, democratic decision-making, popular participation in government and accountability of public officials to the people. As such it has been pursued as a desirable political objective in itself. Although developing country governments have offered a wide range of justification for decentralising, the results have been mixed. Third world governments have faced myriad problems in designing and implementing programmes for decentralising development administration. Even where the programmes have been relatively successful, not all of the anticipated benefits have accrued to either central or local administrative units.[6] Ultimately decentralisation is a political decision and its implementation a reflection of a country's political process.

Assessing decentralisation at its face value — that is, by the degree to which power and responsibility for planning and managing development activities have actually been transferred from central agencies to other organisations — would lead to pessimistic conclusions. For example, in India, despite the attempts to decentralise development planning and administration, the system remains highly centralised even today. The quasi public institutions have actually expanded the power and control of the Central Government at the expense of the local governments. Despite the apparent concern for decentralisation, programmes were centrally created but not linked to established local organisation and sources of political and financial support. As noted, authority is commonly delegated to local governments, but they are not given the resources to perform their new functions. Therefore, local governments still function as bureaucratic instruments of the centre rather than as generators of alternative values, preferences and aspirations.[7]

**Forms of Decentralisation**

Different forms of decentralisation can be distinguished primarily by the extent to which authority to plan, decide and manage is transferred from the Central Government to other organisations and the amount of autonomy the decentralised organisations achieved in carrying out their tasks. Consideration of local government as an instrument of decentralised development is a study of continuing tension between alternative conceptions, ideas and definitions, because these are determined by alternative images in the mind of the observer. These tensions and subsequent confusions underline concepts of decentralised development, but they are always important in understanding local government. It is fairly obvious, but not always made explicit, that local government encompasses a wide variety of structures, roles, and behaviours, a factor that takes on more significance, when it is linked with the concept of decentralisation.

## Institutional Framework for Decentralisation

Along with decentralisation must go institution building. The institutional framework must be such as to ensure integration of local institutions, for determining programmes of development and their implementation. It should ensure interaction with the population or institutions with elected members and other organisations working for development in that area and it should be capable of bringing all these under the control of a single agency and must have adequate mechanism for the formulation of the plan based on local resources, analysis of the felt-needs and the requirements of the area. It should also be in a position to clearly demarcate the spheres for the execution of the development programmes, included in the decentralised plan, at that level. Therefore, an essential pre-requisite for success of decentralised planning at the sub-state or local level is the presence of democratic institutions at grassroot level, endowed with powers, functions and adequate financial resources.

## People's Participation and Decentralisation

One of the strong features of the decentralised planning is that it enables the full involvement of the people in the process of plan formulation and implementation. Everything cannot be done by the government alone. Energies of the people will have to be realised, especially in the rural areas so that they will participate in the development of their area. Therefore, public on popular participation is an essential instrument and this would help in assessing the felt-needs of the people, mobilising local resources for plan implementation, carrying out people's sector, reducing resistance to plan formulation and implementation, stepping up the speed of implementation by mobilising popular support and co-operation. Thus there must be people's participation in decision-making, in implementation, in the delivery of benefits and in the assessment or evaluation of the results.

Decentralised planning can be successful only when popular participation is pursued both as an end and as a means. As an end it is an inevitable extension of the national efforts and commitment to bring the masses into the mainstream of development process for establishing an egalitarian socio-economic order. As a means, popular participation should observe all components and all aspects of development. The institutional problem at the local level is of stimulating and organising direct mass participation among communities and groups as precondition for direct participation at the national level. The specific issue centres on the appropriate institutional framework at the local level to stimulate participation of the people.[8]

Effective popular participation in local decision-making requires national policy decision on a number of issues. First, authority for decision-making over a range of issues must be decentralised in order to give content to local participation. Secondly, legislative changes may be necessary to permit decentralisation to create a local institutional structure wherever necessary and to eliminate any legal barriers to participation. It is at the local level that the tangible results of development strategies can be seen. The effectiveness of development in terms of providing benefits will depend on the effectiveness of these institutions that translate plans into concrete activities. Similarly, the degree to which the problem will contribute to development will depend on the functioning of the local institutions.

### *Indian Experience*

Decentralisation of planning and administration has been on India's agenda since independence but has not been very encouraging. Here we shall analyse only the institutional framework that has been developed in India during the last four decades. During the colonial period, the emphasis was on administration of local areas by centrally recruited and trained personnel, a form that eventually displaced traditional village governance particularly the councils of elders. After independence when the planning process was initiated during the early fifties it was largely a centralised affair. As development proceeded, the importance of and the need for decentralisation was keenly felt. The Planning Commission advocated the concept of planning from below and people's participation in the planning process. In fact the need to decentralise both planning and administration was felt more after the failure of the Community Development and National Extension Service programmes. It was a massive rural reconstruction programme launched by the government of India, but it could not succeed because it remained a bureaucratic programme and failed to evoke any positive response at the local level. People's involvement and participation was lacking. Therefore, to study the causes of the failure of the programme a committee headed by Balwantrai Mehta was appointed. The Committee found that development cannot progress without the devolution of responsibility and power. Community development can be real, only, when the community understands its problems, realises its responsibilities, exercises the necessary power through its chosen representatives and maintains a constant and intelligent vigilance on local administration. It was with this objective that the Committee recommended an early establishment of statutory elective local bodies and devolution on them of the necessary resources, power and authority. The Committee gave a comprehensive blue-print for the creation of a three tier local self-government, known as Panchayati Raj with major tasks viz., developmental, administrative and political being assigned to these institutions. By the 1960's almost all the states had constituted the Panchayats.

*Failure of Panchayats*

However, within a few years of the enactment of Panchayati Raj legislations, within the administrative systems of different states resistance developed and ground began to be cut from under Panchayati Raj Institutions, specially Zilla Parishads through the creation of official bodies headed by the Collector, such as, *District* Development Council, District Planning Board, etc. Transfer of subjects to Panchayati Raj Institutions remained partial and the financial and other delegations needed, remained highly constrained and incomplete. Moreover as these institutions took shape the MLAs, MLCs and other politicians came to realise the strategic importance of Panchayati Raj institutions and started looking at representatives of these institutions as their political rivals. As a result the decline of these institutions started. The performance and objectives of these institutions, were considerably diluted leaving them in a state of directionlessness. The declining political support coupled with indifferent attitude of local level bureaucracy and delay in conduct of elections further led dimmution of the developmental and administrative role of Panchayati Raj institutions, adding insult to the injury.

Decentralisation suffered because of centralisation and the institutional mechanism failed. The search for new bearings began and to suggest new ways and means to revitalise Panchayati Raj institutions, Ashoka Mehta Committee was appointed. Diagnosing the ills afflicting the Panchayati Raj institutions, the Committee pointed out that haphazard programmes, non-performance, rise of vested interests, lack of political will on the part of Central or State Governments, lack of financial resources etc, positively contributed to its decline. At the same time Panchayati Raj itself got lost in the haze of conflicting interpretations. The Committee reviewed the past and presented its recommendations having thrust on functional necessity for decentralisation of administration. The major recommendations of the Committee were; two-tier model of Panchayati Raj i.e. Zilla Parishad and Mandal Panchayat, direct election to both these bodies, reservation of seats for SC/ST and women and devolution of a number of functions to the Panchayats.

Inspite of the recommendations of these two committees the decline of Panchayati Raj institutions continued and the tendency of centralisation prevailed. One of the major outcomes of the past experience with Panchayati Raj institutions, has been that the State Governments have not allowed these institutions to grow. They have never been vested with the powers and functions that they are supposed to enjoy. Therefore a search for a system that would transfer power to the people in real terms was evident. The idea that gained momentum during the late 1980's was to confer constitutional status to Panchayati Raj system.

*Constitutional Status*

Two attempts were made, in the form of Sixty-Fourth Constitutional Amendment and Seventy-Second Constitutional Amendment bills to confer Constitutional status to Panchayats but due to various reasons the attempts failed. It was only in 1993 that the Seventy-Third Constitutional Amendment Act was passed. The new Act aims to institutionalise the Panchayats. It provides for the constitution of the Gram Sabha at the village level and a three-tier system of the village, block and the district level. Seats have been reserved for SC/ST and women. To increase women's participation in the Panchayats, one third of the seats, to be filled up by direct elections, have been reserved in their favour. The terms of Panchayats has been fixed for five years with a provision that in case a panchayat is dissolved it shall be reconstituted within six months.

The legislature of a state may endow the Panchayats with such powers and authority as may be necessary to enable them to function as institutions of self-government. One of the important aspects of the Act is that it provides for the constitution of a Finance Commission to review the financial position of the Panchayats and to suggest measures. This Commission shall be constituted every fifth year by the Governor. Similarly the superintendence, direction and control of all elections to the Panchayats shall be vested in a State Election Commission. The Act also consists of a long list of Scheduled areas that are to be transferred to the Panchayats.

There is no doubt that the Act aims to restore the dignity of the Panchayats but it has certain drawbacks. Firstly too much has been left to the State Governments to decide regarding the powers that are to be given to the Panchayats. Even the Gram Sabhas have not been assigned any specific function under the Act. There is no provision for the recall of the elected representatives. At least this could have been introduced at the village level and the Pradhan would be accountable. The Act also does not provide for the reservation for the minorities. The question is, can any state government do so? There are few points that need to be taken into account.

**Conclusion**

We can conclude that decentralisation is not a quick fix for the administrative, political or economic problems of a country. Given the shortcomings revealed by our experience with decentralisation it can be achieved through a small-scale, incremental transfers of powers and responsibilities especially for the local management functions. Decentralisation must be viewed more realistically, however, not as a general solution to all of the problems of under development, but rather as a range of administrative or organisational devices that may improve the efficiency, effectiveness and responsiveness of various levels of government. The more successful decentralisation efforts are those that are thoroughly prepared and carefully implemented.

There is no doubt that the introduction of the Seventy-Third Constitutional Amendment Act is a welcome step forward in democratic decentralisation. A participatory democracy at the grass-root level is essential for healthy growth of democratic institutions and processes. Besides, the process of development, economic and political, cannot leave the people for whom it is meant on the peripheri and still hope to succeed. However, a structural change of this magnitude in the process of the development cannot succeed unless the process itself is reoriented to allow it to operate meaningfully and flourish. The development process would need to be restructured with emphasis on participative development through mobilisation of local resources, local manpower, appropriate technology and, to the extent, possible self-help. Only then, decentralisation and development is possible.

## REFERENCES

1. Prasad C.S. (1991) : District Planning : An Approach to Decentralised Planning; *The Administrator*, Vol XXXVI, p.39.
2. Rondinelli, D. (1978) : National Investment Planning and Equity Policy in Developing Coutries; The Challenge of Decentralised Administration, *Policy Sciences*, Vol. 10, No. 1, pp. 45-74.
3. See Maddick, H. (1963) : *Democracy, Decentralisation and Development*. Bombay, Asia Publishing House.
4. Rondinelli, D. (1981) : Government, Decentralisation in Comparative Perspective; Theory and Practice in Developing Countries, *International Review of Administrative Sciences*, Vol. 47, No. 2, pp. 133-45.
5. See Uphoff, N. and M. Essman (1974) : Local Organisations for Rural Development in Asia, Itnaca, Cornell University, Centre for International Studies.

6. Cheema, G.S. and D.A. Rondinelli (Ed.) (1983) : *Decentralisation and Development*, Beverly Hills, Sage.
7. Friedman, H. (1983) : Local Political Alternatives for Decentralised Development in Decentralisation and Development (ed.), G.S. Cheema and D.A. Rondinelli, Beverly Hills, Sage.
8. Mishra, Suresh (1992) : Popular Participation and Panchayati Raj; The Indian Experience, *ISDA Journal*, Vol. 2, p. 85.

SEVEN

# STRUCTURAL BASIS OF CHILD LABOUR

BIMAL KUMAR

Childhood is preparatory stage for adulthood. In traditional societies, children were prepared for performance of ascribed traditional occupation. In certain categories of occupation, children learnt it while working with their parents. In the case of elite groups, children were trained by specialised instructors/teachers/preceptors. So child labour has been part of work culture and life systems among the various groups engaged in works based on predominantly human labour and skill such as cultivation or other crafts. Even specialised skills were acquired in the process of work. Thus child labour and skill learning was inseparable among traditional crafts and artisan works. In certain cases children were imparted some reading or writing capabilities – but that was mostly done to inculcate some religious teachings.

On the other hand, recruitment process in the ruling elite structure required that children were trained to control and run a system. Their hegemony was contingent on their capability to organise and motivate individuals to work for the system which they controlled. This required that they were better equipped to control and were capable of applying knowledge for better organisation. Broadly, an elite structure had to perform three functions :firstly, to maintain stability of system, secondly,to expand the system, and thirdly, to compete with other such formations if required. Besides personal excellence, they were supposed to deal with individuals or group of individuals to stabilise and expand the system or social organism to which they belonged. And whenever necessary, make plans to deal with the competitors or adversaries.

Thus in case of general workers, they were required to become proficient in one particular work and socialise under the system or social formation under which they worked. That is why in case of skilled work, they were required to learn the skill from early childhood in order to become skilled worker and imbibe work culture of the system by the time they attained adulthood. Even for a totally unskilled work, a person was engaged in work from early childhood so that he/she was socialised in the work-culture which was conducive with the needs of the system in which he/she worked. On the other hand those who were prepared and trained to enter ruling elite structure underwent specialised trainings and teaching during their childhood. Their childhood learning and activities related to learning were not income generating activities.

Thus child labour and child learning were structurally linked with the social and economic organisation of even traditional societies. If we look at this problem in terms of production relations, it could also be said that workers (such as cultivators, artisans and craftsmen) in the economy engaged their family members in work from early childhood. On the other hand those who lived on the surplus generated by labour or exchange employed teachers/instructors to educate or train their children.

**Growth of Formal Sectors**

The structural basis of child labour underwent a sea-change with the advent of modern era. The modern era began with the advent of organised modern industrial sector in the economic sphere and emergence of nation-states on the political horizon. As a result of these changes, two new factors entered the social life. One was that new occupations (including those in management and bureaucracy) were not related to family or community tradition. Secondly, a new citizen (as distinct from subjects) was sought to be prepared with new loyalty towards modern state. The primordial loyalty of this new citizen had to be subordinated to the over-arching loyality towards the 'new nation-state'.

The system of achieving excellence in any discipline of knowledge itself underwent a radical change. This in turn, also changed the role and scope of imparting knowledge. Various new disciplines of knowledge grew and came to prominence. New discoveries and inventions in areas of science and technology changed the character of economic organisations and production systems. New production systems required systematic knowledge and skill to apply them. This could be imparted through formal and highly professional institutions. Thus formal professions required formal learning and formal training under systematic courses. Thus learning of children and adolscents (even adults) was separated from their working. That is, in the formal sectors, learning and employment do not go together. Obviously, child employment is looked down as the bane of society in development process.

Thus the role of formal education became important. With the economy largely getting covered under the formal sector, employment of workers in formal sectors without having some formal education created disharmony between the traditional values and modern values. Therefore, modern education became a necessary precondition to interact with and enter into modern sectors of economy. It was even more important for those who were to become part of the new elite structure and different organs of state power. The formal education thus became an instrument to bring children out of traditional systems and traditional values. The very nature of formal system of economy and power organs required that children were not allowed to work during their childhood.

**Dualism**

It is true that in developed economies, the formal sector has, by and large, replaced traditional sectors of economy. However, in developing economies the size of modern organised sector continues to remain small and grows slowly. In case of India, informal sectors constitute a very large proportion of its economy. Alongwith the traditional informal sectors which continue to absorb a vast majority of workers, a large new informal sector has also grown with the growth of modern organised sector.

There are two types of persons engaged in the informal sector. One, those who have to interact with and take benefits from the exchange with the formal sectors. This is the category of elites within the informal sector. Some formal education is considered necessary for recruitment in this category.

The other category of persons engaged in the informal sector consists of those workers who work under (or for) these elites. Formal education is not required of these workers. Thus whereas elites in the informal sector go for certain level of formal education and therefore enter work - force at a later age, those who work under (or for) them send to or engage their children in work at an early age.

*Informal sector and the child labour*

Employment of workers in this category of informal sectors is not contingent on any formal education. A certain degree of proficiency in reading, writing and accounting work are indeed important, but beyond that formal education has no significance for them. This level of knowledge could be acquired by working children even while they are engaged in work.

Moreover, skill learning and training in this informal sector begins at quite an early age. In fact child labour and skill learning in the informal sector become two facets of the same process. It does not give any extra benefits to first send children to school and then engage them as workers in the informal sectors after they have passed certain level examination.

Structured parts of economy consists of both formal as well as informal sectors (economy of tribes, nomads etc. constitute the unstructured parts of economy), and therefore informal sector is structurally linked with the total structured economy. However, informal sector is not a homogeneous sector with within sector linkages, common rules or common wage structure. Activities in this sector range from totally unskilled work to highly skilled work; from totally traditional activities to modern activities. Even from employment point of view, activities range from highly unstable employment to very high degree of stable employment.

There is also, therefore, tendency within the informal sector to move from unskilled type of work to semi-skilled and further to skilled type of work. Obviously workers also want to move from low income activity to work which gives them higher income. The combination of these two i.e. skill level and income level determines the social esteem of the worker within informal sector. That is why, low income – unskilled jobs are considered less respectable while high income skilled jobs are respectable jobs for them. Hence, there is a tendency to move from less respectable to respectable jobs.

This status factor within the informal sector is crucial for sending children to work. Parents prefer to send their children to jobs in which child could also learn some skill besides making some earnings. That is why, when income of a family engaged in low type of work in informal sector increases, the family prefers to send the child to skill learning type of work rather than just wage work where child would not learn any skill.

Hence our submission is that, poverty alleviation is important, but it will not automatically put a brake on child labour employment. So long as a large informal sector exists, children would continue to be engaged in work. Very poor parents would be forced to allow children to work in agricultural labour work or herding type of work in rural areas and in shoe-shining, rag-picking or utensil cleaning type of work in urban areas. Parents with relatively higher income would like their children to be employed in such work in which they could learn the skill also. Parents who are themselves engaged in some skilled work (in household industry or with some employer) also engage their children in work to impart skill proficiency amongst them as early as possible.

Thus larger the size of informal sector in the economy, bigger would be the number of child workers in the society, greater would be the heterogeneity in the types of activities in which they are engaged.

**The Colonial Factor**

The transition of India from a traditional system to modern system was not a simple one. This transition was initiated and effected under foreign rule when India was a colony. The colony (i.e.India) was subjected to drain by the empire. The traditional system maintaining stability and equilibrium was disturbed first by direct drain and next by effecting structural changes which made India's economy a dependent economy. These policies resulted in the decline and finally destruction of handicraft in many areas. The traditional land control system and agricultural system was also changed to destroy the autonomy of those systems.

These changes had three major impacts: One, drain could be organised through structural linkage of the colony with the empire. Secondly, the traditional production system and entrepreneurship quality deteriorated very fast, so that adoption of new methods and innovation within the indigenous system became out of question. As a result of this, traditional sectors were further pushed backwards. Thirdly, peasants and artisans were alienated from their productive assets. This not only generated large scale unemployment but also led to proletarianisation and immiserisation of workers. They were no more owner workers, and the status of their children also transformed radically due to this change. Earlier children used to work under the guidance and supervision of parents or other adult members of the family. Participation in household work also strengthened familial bonds and sense of belongingness, besides imparting traditional skill under the parental protection and care. With the alienation of workers from their means of production, children were forced to work for 'others' and thereby made vulnerable for exploitation of all kinds.

II

**Recent Trends**

Efforts to quantify the problem often obfuscates real issues. However, some estimates of the magnitude of child labour is necessary to understand the trend. According to the census data, total number of child workers was 14.49 million in 1961 and 10.74 million in 1971. According to 1981 census there were 13.6 million child workers out of which 11.2 million were main workers and 2.4 million worked as marginal workers. There were still 2.3 million children in the age group (0-14) years who were non-workers but seeking/available for work (table B-9, Census of India 1981). In 1983, the Planning Commission had projected the number of child workers as 17.36 million. However, the finding of the Operations Research Group, Baroda, (published in 1983) estimated that there were 44 million working children in India. This figure is based on an All India Child Labour Survey conducted by the Operations Research Group in 1980-81.

But more important than the overall size of child workers is the change in the structure of child workers in India after 1960s. Two discernible changes have taken place in the structure of child workers during the recent past.

One is that the number of female child workers has increased at a phenomenal rate. In the age group 0-14 years the male population increased by 17.67 per cent, but the number of male child workers decreased by 3.51 per cent. On the other hand, the female population in the age group 0-14 years increased by 17.77 per cent while the number of female child workers increased by 32.23 per cent. This shows that problem of child labour needs to be tackled by concentrating more on female child workers rather than on male child workers.

TABLE 7.1: Growth Rates (per cent) of Population and Main Workers, (1971-81)

| Category | Male | | Females | |
|---|---|---|---|---|
| | population | workers | population | workers |
| 1. Total of all ages | 24.46 | 22.46 | 24.94 | 44.99 |
| 2. (0-14) years | 17.67 | —3.51 | 17.77 | 32.23 |

*Note* : Figures exclude Assam.
*Source* : Census of India, 1981 (Based on 5% sample data).

The other important change which deserves consideration is related to the changes in the occupational structure of child workers. Occupation in which share of child labour has considerably declined are: cultivation declined from 51.11 per cent in 1961 to 36.05 per cent in 1971 and to 35.95 per cent in 1981. Similarly the percentage of child workers engaged in household industry declined from 10.24 per cent in 1961 to 3.15 per cent in 1971 and thereafter increased slightly to 3.79 per cent in 1981.

On the other hand, occupations in which percentage of child workers has significantly increased are : (i) Agricultural Labourers, and (ii) Manufacturing other than household industry. The percentage of child workers who worked as Agricultural Labourers increased from 22.05 per cent in 1961 to 42.72 per cent in 1971 and 42.76 per cent in 1981. Similarly, the percentage of child workers engaged in manufacturing other than household industry increased from 1.66 per cent in 1961 to 2.93 per cent in 1971 and further to 4.84 per cent in 1981.

These findings have a very serious implication. They establish that even after independence, there were a large number of child workers who worked not for others as wage workers, but in the family enterprises both in agriculture and industry. This scenario has radically changed and cultivators have been transformed into agricultural labourers, while those who worked for the household industry have shifted to work as wage labour in manufacturing other than household industry. The process of alienation of owner workers/cultivators from their productive assets, set in motion during the British regime, continued even after attaining Independence.

This in our view, is a qualitative change in the composition of child labour employment. The fact that more and more children are forced to shift from household enterprise to wage work means more and more children are pushed to work in an environment which is bereft of family/humane touch and is more exploitative. Child attitude also significantly change, because in the earlier case they had a satisfaction that they were also owners of their means of production. Alienation from means of production not only signifies immiserisation, but it also represents lowering of their self esteem.

TABLE 7.2: Children Working in Different Areas of Employment in India according to 1971 Census and 1981 Census

| S. No. | Nature of Activity | Distribution of Child Workers in Different Occupation (in %) 1961 | 1971 | 1981 |
|---|---|---|---|---|
| 1 | 2 | 3 | 4 | 5 |
| 1. | Cultivators | 51.11 | 36.05 | 35.95 |
| 2. | Agricultural Labourers | 22.05 | 42.72 | 42.76 |
| 3. | Livestock, Forestry, Fishing Hunting, Plantations etc. | 7.18 | 8.24 | 6.30 |
| 4. | Mining and quarrying | (including mining and quarrying) | 0.22 | 0.23 |
| 5. | Manufacturing processing serving, repairs etc. | 11.90 | 6.08 | 8.63 |
| | (a) Household Industry | 10.24 | 3.15 | 3.79 |
| | (b) Others | 1.66 | 2.93 | 4.84 |
| 6. | Construction | 0.45 | 0.55 | 0.72 |
| 7. | Transport, Storage and Communication | 0.16 | 0.39 | 0.29 |
| 8. | Trade and commerce | 1.06 | 1.97 | 2.20 |
| 9. | Others services | 6.04 | 3.77 | 2.92 |
| | Total number of child workers in the age group 0-14 years (in '000) | 100.00<br>14,489.89 | 100.00<br>10,739.00 | 100.00<br>11,168.00 |

*Note.* In the 1971 census no distinction is made between 'main workers' and 'marginal workers'. In the 1981 census 'main workers' have been defined as those who worked for more than six months. The 1981 Census figures given above relate to 'main workers' only.

## III

Brassware industry, Moradabad and Lock-making Industry of

Aligarh are typical of their own class. They are among the few major industries in Uttar Pradesh where the concentration of child labour is very high.

Structure of these industries comprises both formal segment as well as informal sector segment, wherein both these sectors are closely intertwined. This would become obvious from the description of categories of participants in these industries. These industries consist of broadly three types of participants in the production structure. These are : (i) Brand-owner manufacturers, or registered manufacturers; (ii) Middle-men contractors; and (iii) Artisans who work on order or as skilled craftsmen in workshops.

Registered/brandowner manufacturers fall in the category of organised sector, while artisans, are by and large in the informal sector. Most of the artisans run their own processing units which are unregistered household units. They generally receive work orders from middlemen contractors, who work, as link between registered manufacturers and artisans. Both lock-making in Aligarh and brassware work in Moradabad were originally done by rural artisans. Like many other traditional occupations, boys of the household in these works were also engaged since early childhood. With the growth of these industries, Aligarh and Moradabad towns became the central location of these respective industries. In the process poor of various backward and depressed castes/communities joined these industries. They also acquired the skill and became good craftsmasters. Market competition forced many small artisan producers to join the ranks of skilled labours or contract artisans who worked on order from contractors or industrialists. Some small and medium scale producers became middle-men contractors also for large registered manufacturers.

Secondly, the competition among artisans to secure work has increased manifold due to rise in the number of artisans. Registered manufacturers and middlemen-contractors tend to take advantage of this situation. On the other hand, since artisans had neither knowledge about market conditions, nor they are in a position to influence it, they are unable to take advantage when market demands could favour them. As a result of this registered manufacturers and contractors are able to deal with them by offering the minimum amount of contract, irrespective of market conditions.

Due to low contract wage, artisans were forced to employ

family child labour or hired labour to keep the expenses on labour at the minimum in order to make some earnings for themselves.

Thus, it was the informal segment of these industries which was responsible for high concentration of child labour in these industries.

*Informalisation of Formal Units*

An important fall out of such structure of production was that even registered units tried to function as informal sector units. In order to avoid the application of Factories Act, 1948, many manufacturers had deliberately split their firms into smaller processing units/workshops, and dispersed them in different locations. Not only this, even those artisans who owned single processing units, were made part of the production channel of registered manufacturers. Artisans were not employed, but an arrangement had been made in which they worked on contract basis. That way, they could be called self-employed. But they received orders, input materials as well as advances from manufacturers through middlemen contractors, which made these artisans totally dependent on them. Manufacturers are in a position to employ these artisans in their own factories if they so wished. But then it would not be possible to employ child labour and get the work done at low wage-cost. Hence the arrangement in which artisans remain outside the formal segment of these industries. Thus, *de facto* these artisans could be said to be workers of the formal segment, but *de jure*, they constitute the informal segment of these industries.

It was because of the existence of a very large informal sector segment in these industries that there was high concentration of child labour in these industries.

Another aspect of the families who sent their children to work was that they were traditionally engaged in activities which fall in the category of informal sector. Their work culture and attitude towards child labour had grown out of that structure. In our study of families of child labourers in lock-making industry (Aligarh) as well as brassware industry (Moradabad), we found that present day adult workers of these families had also entered work-force when they were children. Indeed, parents were found to be aware of the need to send children to school. They considered that knowledge of reading, writing and accounting work was necessary in their day to day dealings. Yet they sent their children to work. The most obvious reason suggested for this was that there was need for supplementary income in the family. Nevertheless, they also said that working children were in the process of learning skill and therefore there was nothing wrong in sending them to such work. They also suggested that actual employment period of children would start when they become artisans in their own right.

It was also found that in cases where poverty was the main cause for sending children to work, children were sent to work between the age of 3 to 6 years. While those families which viewed child's engagement in work as period of skill learning and apprenticeship sent their children to work between 10 to 14 years of age. It was also found that only very poor parents sent their children to hazardous works.

Thus even the better-off parents felt that period of work during childhood was the period of learning skill. Since no formal system of skill training was available to them they engaged their children in skill oriented work, so that they could become independent artisans by 18 years or so. Another remarkable finding was that even working children liked their work, wanted to remain in employment and become full-fledged artisans after four or five years of working as 'helpers'.

So even those industries where formal sector has informalised its production system, the concentration of child labour is very high. Instead of deriving benefits of the formal sector, these activities are webbed with all the characteristics prevailing in the informal sector.

## IV

There is a plethora of documentation to establish that families which sent their children to work were poor families. Many surveys also revealed that child workers generally belonged to backward/lower castes. In many traditional crafts children from Muslim Community were in predominance. Besides these social factors there are some other characteristics of such families also. For example adult underemployment, large family size, illiteracy, low wages etc. Some social evils have also been reported among these families, such as alcoholism, gambling, etc.

**The Social Factor**

We have discussed that because of the specific social structure in India, the problem of child labour has both a caste dimension as well as gender dimension. Child labourers come mostly from backward and depressed castes and Muslim artisan castes. Similarly, we have also seen that whereas number of male child workers was declining, the number of female child workers was increasing.

So given these facts, any strategy to banish child labour must also take into account these factors as well. Let us, for example, consider the aspect of education. Concerted and special measurers must be taken to make education available and economically viable for families of such categories. Even though we come across such cases also in which a child was sent to work at the age of three or four years. But generally children's age of entry into work force has been found to be 7 or 8 years. Whatever, the age at which a child starts the work, usually a child is found to become whole time worker only after 8 years of age. So in most of the cases, a child could be drawn into part time or non-formal type of education upto the age of 8 years. This means that the age-group of (3-8) years could be targeted for education of children who are (or likely to become) a child labour. The practical implication of such a situation is that primary education of such a situation is that primary education of all sorts (formal, non-formal, vocational etc.) should be vigorously pursued among children of these communities. The problem of working children is, therefore, also related to problem of social inequality as well.

The social inequality angle of child labour could be addressed if economic factors are not left entirely on the mercy of market forces. On the one hand a deliberate effort is needed to be made for socially disadvantaged group, to bring them in the economic mainstream. On the other, social awakening and education for such groups should be planned at a very large scale.

*Other Characteristics*

Let us now discuss other characteristics related to child labour. As already mentioned, these include adult underemployment, large family size, illiteracy, low wages etc. But all such characteristics are part of the structure in which children work. In such structural relationship, it is difficult to delineate causal relationship between these factors.

In fact these factors reinforce each other in the structural millieu in which they work. For example, relation between poverty and large family size and its impact on children. Due to acute poverty parents are unable to feed their children. Therefore, they force their children to share the economic burden of the family. If they had less children then they might had to bear less burden. That is, large size of family reduces per capita income, which in turn reduces their per capita consumption. It means that their poverty would be less pinching if they adopt to small family norm. This argument is impeccable if viewed in isolation from the structure within which these factors work. However, there is another dimension of the structure within which these factors operate. Under this dimension, a child means an additional income to the family. For the poorer sections of society more the children, more would be the earning. Thus for them children represent economic benefits. There are many studies which show the positive correlation between child labour and fertility. The main inference of these studies is that an economic structure where child labour plays an important role is conducive to high fertility. So it is not the size of family that determines the extent of child labour, but the economic structure that absorbs child labour is responsible for large family sizes.

Under-employment of adults is another factor, which is attributed for incidence of child labour. In a way, child labour may be the consequence as well as the cause of adult unemployment or underemployment. With the entry of child workers, the demand of adult workers declines. Child worker participation also lower the bargaining power of adult workers. Once adult workers start to work on lower wages, their family income further decreases. This further compels them to send their children to work in order to supplement family income. Thus child labour and adult un(der)employment reinforce each other in the economic structure which is characterised by low cost, low wage, low productivity syndrome. Thus poverty, un(der)employment, illiteracy, large family size, child labour - all these factors are characteristics of an economic structure functioning under the informal sector. No one factor could be attributed as cause of other factors. In fact each of these is the product of the economic structure which is characterised by low cost, low wage and low productivity syndrome. In such a structure each factor such as poverty, un(der)employment, illiteracy, large family size, child labour reinforces every other factor.

Another aspect of the problem of child labour is that it is generally analysed for structured parts of economy only. But lately alienation of communities in the unstructured part of economy is also seriously aggravating the problem of child labour in many parts of the country. Tribals and nomads had been living on natural resources for centuries. As their access and freedom to utilise such natural resources is fast declining, these communities are fast adding to the ranks of child workers in many activities. There are many reports which suggest that tribals who had been alienated from forests are working in quarrying or brick-kiln type of works. It has been reported that all the family members of a tribal family including women and children are put/stayed near such work-places and work as more or less as captive labourers. They are also reported to be engaged in construction activities in certain areas. So it is not unlikely that they would spread to other activities as well.

## Conclusion

We have tried to underline the structural basis of prevalence of child labour in Indian economy. There is already great international pressure on India to contain employment of child workers. Even non-governmental fora in the west are propagating to boycott the products of industries which employ child labour.

There have been serious efforts to eradicate employment of child labour in organised and in some semi-organised sectors only. But our understanding of structural basis of child labour tells us that piece-meal and adhoc policies would not be effective. But even more important issue in this respect is that whether the IMF conditionality supported macro policies of liberalisation and marketisation would help us in overcoming these structural problems or not.

The process of liberalisation, as is being pursued, may lead to abdication of its responsibility by the state to monitor resource distribution among different sectors of economy. Market-forces' free interplay provides best results only when all sectors of economy work and grow under a common institutional framework. However, as of now, formal sectors and informal sectors of Indian economy work under different types of institutional arrangements. Under these circumstances present day type of market forces would, at the most, help only formal sectors of the economy. Informal sector of economy would most likely be affected adversely under the free play of so called market forces. If the condition of informal sector deteriorates, while formal sector is not able to absorb labour at a large scale, then the problem of child labour may further escalate under the impact of the policy of liberalisation. The basis of our fear lies in the fact that displacement of labour will take place at a very large scale in the short run. In the mean while, size of labour force will continue to increase, at least during the next one decade (Any perceptible impact of decline in population growth rate would affect the rate of increase in labour force size only after a decade or so).

The structural adjustment programme will, at the most, take care of those workers who are displaced from large/ organised industries.

Thus, there are three distinct possibilities which emerge from this scenario : (i) shrinkage of employment opportunities; (ii) closure of smaller units due to lack of protection, which would entail large scale unemployment or underemployment; and (iii) shrinkage of employment opportunity on the one hand and increasing size of labour force on the other would aggravate the problem of underemployment beyond socially tolerable limits.

Naturally, these situations would force affected families to engage their children also in the work. Even otherwise, the informal sector had been, generally, a low income generating sector. We have also seen that, in terms of economic categories, the number of child labour had been increasing among ; (i) agricultural labourers, and (ii) non-household manufacturing sector.

Among the social categories, backward castes, Muslims and women account for the overwhelming majority of child workers. By and large, these categories refer to non-asset owning or little asset owning sections of the society.

If we are seriously concerned to eradicate the blot of child labour from our society, a two pronged strategy will have to be worked out and pursued. At one level structural base of the economy will be required to be reorganised so that informal sectors as well as tribal economy also become equal partners in the mainstream economy. Notwithstanding the differences in institutional arrangements of these economies, these sectors must be made remunerative and non-exploitative.

The other level of action should constitute the strategy of direct attack on child labour incidence. Such a strategy will have to be family based, but at the same time caste/community specific, gender specific and area specific.

In the light of our investigations in lock-making industry, Aligarh and Brassware industry, Moradabad, we would suggest that instead of a few special schools, two types of schools should be run at a very large scale. The present system of general schools for children should continue and constitute one type. However, now henceforth, greater emphasis should be placed in opening vocational schools at a very large scale. Children who join work-force, could not be expected to study upto higher levels. Therefore, vocational schools, which give education upto Vth standard level or its equivalent, should be the focal point for drawing potential working children within the purview of vocational education system.

As regards the general upliftment of affected families, the present policy is simply based on increasing budgetary allocations for different target oriented and rural development programmes. Even the talk of increasing productivity of labour and upgradation of technology in informal sectors are done in a very casual and ritualistic way. There is no long-term perspective for small/traditional sectors. Allocations for research and development activities in these sectors were meagre even earlier. With the new policy of encouraging direct foreign investment, R&D is likely to suffer even in the organised sector, but the hopes for R&D in small and traditional sectors have almost completely waned. Unless a strong R&D base is developed for small/traditional sectors of economy which constitute the non-formal sectors of economy, problems like child labour, low wages, low productivity etc. — which emanate from present day structure of informal sector would remain unresolved.

EIGHT

# IMPACT OF ICDS PROGRAMMES ON WOMEN AND CHILD DEVELOPMENT IN ALLAHABAD DISTRICT : A Case Study

S.K. PANT

Of late, there has been a growing awareness, around the world that the success of any development programme, be it a national or a regional, depends not only on its natural resources but also on its human resources that is why all nations are placing increasing stress on their manpower planning.

## Probable Heads

The investments on health, nutrition, education, sanitation etc. are some of the probable heads that tend to bring forth substantial improvement (both quantitatively as well as qualitatively) in the efficiency of human beings.

## Indian Expereince

Unfortunately India had a very bad legacy to inherit at the time of Independence when wide spread poverty, illiteracy, malnutrition were rampant on the one hand and the poor state of infrastructure (both the economic and social) ruled the roost. Therefore, in order to set the things in right order, the country switched to planning soon after attaining political independence.

The impact of planned development has been a mixed one. While the country has emerged out of its shadows in most of the fields where its achievements have received world wide accolades, it has also met with little success in some of the other fields and the development of women and children has been one such area. This is the situation despite the fact that during all these years the country has launched host of programmes for alleviating the hardships of poor and down trodden classes including the women and children.

### Casual Factors

Besides factors like prevalence of abject poverty and patriachal social system which accords a very low social position to women and children, it has been found that in the absence of proper monitoring and coordination, these schemes have worked in complete isolation with each other, often overlapping each other area of coverage thereby blunting the main thrust of the programme.

### Magnitude of the Problem

India has around 127 million[1] children who are said to be below the age of six years and a majority of them are said to be living in the extreme conditions of poverty. The infant mortality rate, one of the crucial indicators of child survivals, continues to be as high as 84 (1991)[2]; 33 per cent (1990)[3] of infants are born with low birth rate and nearly two-fifth of deaths occur in the age group of 0-6 years. Even the target of providing universal primary education fell haywards as the drop out rate at the primary's level continues to be as high as 47.0 per cent (1988).[4]

### Government Endeavours

The perusal of government's efforts towards women and child development dates back to the inception of planning. However, during the first three Five Year Plans, women and child development did not figure prominently and their development was entrusted to voluntary organisations. It was during these years, the formation of Central Social Welfare Board (CSWB) also took place in 1953 with the basic objectives of promoting child welfare programmes and providing assistance to voluntary organisations. The Board also initiated various programmes that covered health, nutrition and education for child development but these efforts were too feeble and insufficient to take on the problem of that magnitude. It was only towards the

Fourth Five Year Plan that an integrated nutrition programme was introduced and since then programmes like Mid-Day Meal (MDM) in 1962-63, Applied Nutrition Programme (ANP) in 1960 and later extended to all states in 1973. Specific Nutrition Programmes (SNP) in 1970-71 have been launched which finally precipitated into the formation of a very ambitious programme known as the Integrated Child Development Scheme (ICDS) in 1975.

**The ICDS**

The ICDS project was launched on experimental basis in 33 community development blocks on Oct.2, 1975 to commemorate the birth anniversary of Mahatma Gandhi. It broadly aims to provide children from poor sections, a packages of basic services like that of health, supplementary nutrition and non-formal pre-school education for a better start in life. More specifically it aims:

(i) to improve the nutritional and health status of children in the age group of 0-6 years;
(ii) to lay the foundation of proper psychological, physical and social development of the child;
(iii) to reduce the incidence of mortality, morbidity and school drop outs;
(iv) to achieve effective coordination of policy and implementations; and
(v) to enhance the capacity of the mother to look after the normal health and nutrition needs through proper nutrition and health education.

Towards achieving these objectives a package of services is rendered essentially through the *anganwadi* worker at the village level centre called *anganwadi*. These packages of services include

- supplementary nutrition
- immunization
- health checkups
- referral services
- treatment of minor ailments
- nutrition and health education to women

- pre-school education to children in the age-group of 3-6 years
- convergence of other support services like water supply, sanitation etc.

*Over View of ICDS Programmes*

Ever since its inception, the ICDS programmes have generated a lot of interest among academicians, planners, administrators and those responsible for implementing the programme. Consequently, a large number of research studies have been conducted to evaluate and assess the impact of the programme on the beneficiaries. The Planning Commission; All India Institute of Medical Sciences, New Delhi; UNICEF etc., to name a few, are some of the organisations that have closely monitored the progress of ICDS at various point of time. A perusal of these studies reveals that while a majority of them have concentrated on health and nutrition components of the scheme, there have also been attempts to study the pre-schooling component of the scheme as well.

The evaluation of Programme Evaluation Organisation (PEO) of Planning Commission in 1976 and a repeat survey in 1977-78 shows that the programme has overcome the initial difficulties such as recruitment of staff, training, equipment supplies but the success of programme has been more in respect of children belonging to the age group of 3-6 years than towards the children belonging to 0-3 years. Like-wise the periodic assessments of AIIMS, New Delhi (1978 and 1981) have also pointed out that the nutritional status and health standards of the children have remarkably improved in the project areas. Similarly, the study conducted by UNICEF (1983) has reported positive attributes of the schemes such as substantial enrollment of Scheduled Castes and Scheduled Tribes children as beneficiaries.[5]

The performance appraisal of Mid-Day Meal (MDM) programme clearly shows that it has failed to reveal any significant increase in the level of enrollment and attributes lack of continuity in the supply of food material to the feeding centres, pilferage in the channels of distribution, non-adherence to minimum number of feeding days and absence of other services like health. Similarly, the Applied Nutrition Programme (ANP) too has not been successful in generating desired level of awareness for the production and consumption of protective foods. The scheme for setting up poultry units and pisciculture could not make much headway due to inadequate health cover and poor management. Moreover, the participation by the Panchayati Raj institutions and Mahila Mandals was extremely poor as they were not fully involved. Even the criteria for selecting the blocks, villages and the beneficiaries, at times were not taken into account.

*Overall Assessment*

Thus it could be said that the impact of the programme according to the studies has been a mixed one. While it has been broadly accepted that it has generated conducive impact on the beneficiaries, it has, somehow, failed to take off beyond the project areas. The ICDS was conceived as the community based programme. It was envisaged that the people's participation would come forth readily in the implementation. However, contrary to the conception, it has acquired a profile of a governments programme and people accepted it as a dole.

*Objectives*

The study attempts to evaluate the performance of the programme in Allahabad district. More specifically, it aims to study the role of *anganwadi* centres in tackling issues like the incidence of malnutrition, morbidity and pre-school education, identify factors supposed to be militating against their scope and also suggest appropriate measures to make these centres more effective.

**The District**

The district of Allahabad lies between latitude 24° 47 and 25° 47′ north longitude 81° 19′ and 82° 29′ east. The length of the district from east to west is about 117 kms. and the breadth from north to south is about 101 kms. and covers an area of 7,261 sq.kms. The population density of the district as per 1991 census was 676 per sq. km. and the sex ratio is 877 females per 1,000 males. The number of literates of the district was worked to be 16.61 lakhs of which the male and females percentage was 47.3 and 18.49 respectively.[6]

Topographically, the district may be divided into three parts — the Trans Ganga Tract or the Ganga Par Plain, the Doab and the Trans Yamuna Tract or the Yamuna Par Plain. These are formed by two main rivers, the Ganga and the Yamuna.

Administratively, the district could be classified into 9 tahsils and 28 development blocks.

The district's economy is primarily agricultural and absorbs about 69.12 per cent of the labour force while the household industry and other workers share being 5.52 per cent and 25.36 per cent as per 1981 census. The main source of irrigation in the district are canals and tube-wells.

## Social Amenities in Rural Areas

The rural areas of the district are made up of 3,9514 revenue villages out of which 3,514 are inhabited. Two-thirds of the rural population of the district lives in the villages having one or more educational institutions, one-fifth of the rural population of the district is in position to avail themselves of medical facilities within the villages. Like wise, one-fourth of rural population too has accessibility to potable water facility. There are about 111 branches of banks in rural areas as per 1981 census.

## The ICDS Programme

The ICDS programme was introduced in the district in the year 1976-77 in only one block viz. Shankergarh where it was proposed to open up 148 *anganwadi* centres . The profile of the *anganwadi* centres in the district has been presented in Table 8.1. It could be seen that the scheme multiplied in subsequent years as more and more blocks were brought into its ambit. The scheme, by the end of 1984-85 was operating in the following four blocks viz. Shankergarh, Meja, Jasra and Kanaili besides one city ward where about 530 *anganwadi* centres were earmarked to be set up.

In the following two years i.e. 1986-87, two more blocks namely Sirathu and Chail were also included in the scheme where another set of 270 *anganwadi* centres was proposed to be set up. More and more blocks of the district were covered in this scheme and by the end of 1989-90 the scheme besides operating in 9 blocks also covered two city wards where in all

1221 *anganwadi* centres were proposed to be set up. Initially, the intake capacity of these centres for women and children was 20 and 64 each of which the number of pregnant and lactating mothers was 11 and 9. Like wise of the total children, the number of those falling between 0 to 3 years and those between 3 to 6 years was 20 and 42 respectively.

TABLE 8.1 : Profile of ICDS Scheme in Allahabad District

| S.No. | Year | Blocks Selected | *Anganwadi* Centres Proposed |
|---|---|---|---|
| 1 | 1976-77 | Shankergarh | 148 |
| 2 | 1980-81 | City-I | 115 |
| 3 | 1982-83 | Meja | 95 |
| | | Jasra | 100 |
| 4 | 1984-85 | Kainali | 72 |
| 5 | 1986-87 | Sirathu | 153 |
| | | Chail | 117 |
| 6 | 1988-89 | City-II | 100 |
| | | Chaka | 104 |
| 7 | 1989-90 | Manjhanpur | 99 |
| | | Saraswasn | 118 |
| | TOTAL | 11 | 1221 |

*Source* : District Information Office, Allahabad

TABLE 8.2: *Anganwadi* Centres, Child and Female Enrollment and Basic Facilities

| S. No. | Name of the Scheme | *Anganwadi* Centres | | | Child Attendence | | Female Attendence | | Facilities | |
|---|---|---|---|---|---|---|---|---|---|---|
| | | S | W | % | Number | % | Number | % | D/W | Toilet |
| 1 | BVP MEJA | 86 | 85 | 98.8 | 5620 | 103.3 | 1305 | 76.7 | – | – |
| 2 | BVP SIRATHU | 153 | 148 | 96.7 | 6808 | 71.9 | 2346 | 79.3 | – | – |
| 3 | BVP JASRA | 151 | 151 | 100.0 | 6906 | 71.5 | 2316 | 76.7 | – | – |
| 4 | BVP CITY-I | 115 | 114 | 99.1 | 5239 | 71.8 | 1824 | 80.0 | – | 78.9 |
| 5 | BVP CITY-II | 100 | 98 | 98.0 | 5812 | 92.7 | 1567 | 79.9 | – | 94.9 |
| 6 | BVP CHAIL | 117 | 107 | 91.5 | 3532 | 51.6 | 1538 | 71.9 | – | |
| 7 | BVP MANJHANPUR | 99 | 74 | 74.7 | 2262 | 47.8 | 1132 | 76.5 | – | – |
| 8 | BVP KANAILI | 72 | 65 | 90.3 | 3916 | 94.1 | 1280 | 98.5 | – | – |
| 9 | BVP SARSAWASN | 118 | 116 | 98.3 | 7424 | 100.0 | 2320 | 100.0 | – | – |
| 10 | BVP CHAKA | 104 | 103 | 99.0 | 6588 | 99.9 | 2047 | 99.4 | – | – |
| 11 | BVP SHANKERGARH | 109 | 106 | 97.2 | 4752 | 70.0 | 1649 | 77.8 | – | – |
| GRAND TOTAL | | 1224 | 1167 | 95.3 | 58859 | 78.8 | 19324 | 82.8 | – | 183 |

*Source*: District Information Office, Allahabad
*Note*: D/W — Drinking Water
S — Sanctioned
W — Working

**Performance Appraisal**

The performance of *anganwadi* centres could be evaluated on the basis of the performance of *anganwadi* centres, the nodal point through which the scheme operates. Hence the performance of *anganwadi* centres is a crucial indicator in determining to what extent the scheme operating be termed successful or a disappointing failure. The performance of these centres in Allahabad district has been a mixed one. The number of *anganwadi* centres sanctioned and subsequently operating, the basic facilities they provide and the proportion of female and children regularly attending these centres have been summarised in Table 8.2.

The study of the Table 8.2 shows that even though these centres have been operating at the sub optimal level, they have succeeded in generating an all round interest and enthusiasm among the rural folks as has been depicted by their proportionately higher rate of enrollment. It could be seen that, on an average, the proportion of children and women attending these centres regularly was over 78 per cent and 82 per cent respectively. In the following two blocks viz. Meja and Sarsawan and also Chaka to some extent, the daily attendance level was cent per cent for children only reflects its growing popularity in the rural areas even though the centres have practically no provision for safe drinking water and only a little over 15 per cent of the total having access to toilet facility. Now, if viewed against this back-drop, the performance of these centres cannot altogether be condemned. The proportion of children and likewise the females regularly attending these centres could receive a further fillip if these centres are provided better facilities to attune themself of tackling problems assigned to them effectively.

*Immunization Coverage*

However, in the field of immunization, the centres performance has not been quite remarkable and these centres have come under severe attack. According to their monthly reports of 1991 and 1992, the total number of females who were provided the immunization cover was 2529 (of which the number of pregnant women being 1463). Now if the total intake capacity of each is 20, the total number is somewhat of the order of 23,340 for the whole of the district which literally implies that the proportion of females receiving immunization coverage being a little over 10 per cent (10.84 per cent to be precise). This extreme low percentage of female immunization may also be attributed, primarily, to the females' non-familiarity with the advantages associated with the use of immunization which requires change in the rural folks perception and approach towards immunization. Secondly, it was also found that immunization is taken up with the active collaboration of other departments like health. It was also found that the department of health did not take up the immunization programmes in the newly inducted blocks and generally followed up a year or two later as was their policy, as a result of which the performance of these centres suffered. It is worth mentioning here that the health department did not participate in the immunization campaign in at least the following two blocks viz. Sarsawan and Maharajganj as the blocks have been recently brought under the scheme and so far there have been no incidence of immunization.

The pattern of immunization coverage to children has been summarised in Table 8.3.

TABLE 8.3 : Immunization Coverage of Children below 6 Years in Allahabad District

| Sl. No. | Particulars | I Dose | II Dose | III Dose | Sub total |
|---|---|---|---|---|---|
| 1 | TT | 1471 (60.26) | 970 (39.74) | – | 2441 (13.30) |
| 2 | BCG | 2926 | – | – | 2926 (15.94) |
| 3 | MEASLES | 2360 | – | – | 2360 (12.85) |
| 4 | DPT | 2133 (40.80) | 1798 (34.39) | 1297 (24.81) | 5228 (28.47) |
| 5 | POLIO | 2284 (45.99) | 1505 (30.31) | 1177 (23.70) | 4966 (27.05) |
| 6 | DPT (BOOSTER) | 209 | – | – | 209 (1.14) |
| 7 | POLIO (BOOSTER) | 102 | – | – | 102 (0.56) |
| 8 | DT | 128 | – | – | 128 (0.70) |
| | GRAND TOTAL | 11613 (63.25) | 4273 (23.27) | 2474 (13.48) | 18360 (31.19) |

*Source:* District Information Office, Allahabad
*Note:* Figures in the Bracket Denote Percentage.

It could be seen that so far the total number of children below the age group of 6 years who were immunized was 18,360 which comes to a little over 31 per cent of the total children attending these anganwadi centres regularly. Further, the study also shows that a little over 13 per cent of this were immunized against tetanus toxide, another just under 16 per cent against the BCG, a little over 15 per cent against measles and just under 29 per cent against DPT while the proportion of those immunized against polio was worked to be a little over 27 per cent and this proportion dipped further to just over one per cent when it came to administering the booster dozes of DPT and polio vaccines which clearly speaks of the limited success the immunization has achieved so far. Another fact the study reveals is the sharp drop in the proportion of beneficiaries when it comes to receiving second or the third round dozes or that of the booster dozes. It could be seen that about 60 per cent of the children received the first round immunization doze for TT but its proportion dipped to just under 40 per cent when it came to receiving the second round doze. Like wise in the case of DPT the proportion of beneficiaries receiving first round of doze was a little over 40 per cent which subsequently came down to under 29 percentage and further down to under 23 per cent when it came to receiving third round of dozes.

*Pre-Schooling*

These centres are also supposed to be imparting pre-school education to the childrens' of 3 to 6 years of age group. As the intake capacity of these centres for this section of students being 42, the total number of children attending centre was estimated to be 49,104 against the official statistics of 46,880 which comes to a little over 95 per cent. The study shows, here too, the boys outpassed the girls as their subsequent proportion was worked out to be over 56 per cent against the girls proportion of 43 per cent.

**Supplementary Nutrition and Incidence of Mal-Nutrition**

Another area where these centres have met with little success, despite maintaining a high level of distributing of supplementary nutrition, has been towards mitigating the incidence of malnutrition. The proportion of beneficiaries receiving the supplementary nutrition and the incidence of malnutrition has been presented in Table 8.4.

The study shows that even though the proportion of beneficiaries (both male and female) who had received supplementary nutrition was high, the problem of incidence of malnutrition still persisted. It could be seen that, on an average, a little over 96 per cent of the children were given supplementary nutrition by these *anganwadi* centres and at least in the following six blocks viz. Sirathu, City-I and City-II, Jasra, Sarsawan and Shankergarh the distribution of supplementary nutrition was cent per cent to females and like wise in the following five blocks, the distribution of supplementary to children was cent per cent. These blocks were Jasra, City-I, City-II, Kanaili and Chaka. All this points out to the fact that despite suffering form several limitations, these centres have performed their task quite admirably and if the problem of malnutrition persisted, it was probably because of many other factors like that of poverty, low intake of cereals and food articles etc.

TABLE 8.4 : Incidence of Malnutrition and Frequency of Supplementary Nutrition

| Sl. No. | Name of the Scheme | Malnourished Child (%) | | Supp-Nutrti. to Benefi. (%) | |
|---|---|---|---|---|---|
| | | Severely | Moderately | Females | Children |
| 1 | BVP MEJA | 0.31 | 3.22 | 99.90 | 88.90 |
| 2 | BVP SIRATHU | 0.14 | 3.11 | 100.00 | 99.90 |
| 3 | BVP JASRA | 0.26 | 4.27 | 106.60 | 100.00 |
| 4 | BVP CITY-I | 0.14 | 3.20 | 100.00 | 100.00 |
| 5 | BVP CITY-II | 0.19 | 3.14 | 100.00 | 100.00 |
| 6 | BVP CHAIL | 0.27 | 3.98 | 0.00 | 83.90 |
| 7 | BVP MANJHANPUR | 0.15 | 3.69 | 99.90 | 88.90 |
| 8 | BVP KANAILI | 0.13 | 3.10 | 99.90 | 100.00 |
| 9 | BVP SARSAWAN | 0.11 | 3.58 | 100.00 | 99.90 |
| 10 | BVP CHAKA | 0.12 | 3.13 | 99.90 | 100.00 |
| 11 | BVP SHANKERGARH | 0.16 | 4.54 | 102.80 | 94.20 |
| | Grand Total | 0.17 | 3.63 | 92.70 | 96.50 |

*Source*: District Information Office, Allahabad

The study also reveals that sizeable proportion of children is suffering from severe and moderate malnutrition. It could be seen that, on an average, 0.17 per cent of children suffered from severe malnutrition and about 3.63 per cent of the total children were moderately malnourished. The following blocks had a high incidence of malnourished children viz. Meja, Jasra and Chail whereas the proportion of children suffering from moderate manourishment was uniformly high all throughout. All this points towards the high magnitude of the problem and is certainly not a reflection of the futility of the scheme.

**Probable Factors**

The analysis clearly shows that so far that these AW centres have not been able to perform upto the expectations and that their performance suffers from many lacunae. Some of the factors thought to be interfering with their day to day working have been summarised as :

(i) *Poor Centre – Population Ratio*

The ICDS scheme, when it was conceived, was envisaged to cover population of 1,000 mark in the normal course and 750 mark for tribal and hill areas, which implies that there should be one centre each for one thousand persons. But so far no where has this standard ratio been maintained. In the case of Allahabad, where this scheme became operational way back in 1976, this ratio, based on the 1981 census projections, was worked out to be over 3253 persons which is more than three times the laid down ratio and this ratio assumes a more critical dimensions at the intra district levels.

(ii) *Lack of Basic Facilities*

The study also reveals that these centres lacked basic facilities like that of toilet and drinking water uniformly except for those centres which were situated in city wards jurisdiction as a result of which the females attendance suffered adversely. This lack of facility also limited the scope of these centres towards imparting health, hygiene and sanitary education which forms a crucial part of their curriculum.

(iii) *Understaffing Syndrome*

Another plausible factor accounting for relative low performance of these centres and featuring prominently in the analysis has been the high incidence of understaffing. The pattern of staffing in these centres has been summarised in

Table 8.5.

The study shows that even at the BVP officer's level, who is the nodal officer coordinating the activities and holding a responsible position, there has been as many as 8 post accounting to a little over 72 per cent, that were of non-regular cadre. This tendency of keeping things at abeyance cast an adverse impact on the efficiency and performance of these responsible officers. Similarly, at the Mukhya Sevikas level, the level of understaffing was observed to be over 61 per cent which varied from a little over 28 per cent in Sirathu block to cent per cent in Sarsawan block. Even at the level of Trained Karyakatries, the problem of understaffing, on an average, was found to over 10 per cent which climbed to much higher proportions at the intra block levels.

TABLE 8.5 : Under Staffing Pattern and Frequency of Supplementary Nutrition

| Sl. No. | Name of the Scheme | BVP Officer | | Mukhya Sevika | | Trained Karya Katri | | Frequency of Supplementary Nutition |
|---|---|---|---|---|---|---|---|---|
| | | R | NR | S | W | S | W | |
| 1 | BVP MEJA | – | 1 | 5 | 2 (40.0) | 85 | 81 (95.3) | Broken Between Oct. '91-Jan. '92 |
| 2 | BVP Sirathu | 1 | – | 7 | 2 (28.6) | 148 | 134 (90.5) | -do- |
| 3 | BVP Jasra | – | 1 | 8 | 4 (50.0) | 151 | 140 (92.7) | -do- |
| 4 | BVP City-I | 1 | – | 5 | 2 (40.0) | 114 | 93 (81.6) | -do- |
| 5 | BVP City-II | - | 1 | 4 | 2 (50.0) | 98 | 95 (96.9) | -do- |
| 6 | BVP Chail | – | 1 | 6 | 2 (33.3) | 107 | 99 (92.5) | -do- |
| 7 | BVP Manjhanpur | - | 1 | 4 | 2 (50.0) | 74 | 57 (77.0) | -do- |
| 8 | BVP Kanaili | – | 1 | 4 | 2 (50.0) | 65 | 62 (95.4) | -do- |
| 9 | BVP Sarsawan | – | 1 | 6 | – | 116 | 84 (72.4) | -do- |
| 10 | BVP Chaka | 1 | – | 5 | 3 (60.0) | 97 | (94.2) | -do- |
| 11 | BVP Shankergarh | - | 1 | 5 | 2 (40.0) | 106 | 104 (98.1) | -do- |
| | Grand Total | 3 | 8 | 59 | 23 (38.9) | 1167 | 1046 (89.6) | |

*Source* : District Information Office, Allahabad

*Note* : Figures in the Bracket Denote Percentage

(iv) *Non–Regular Supply of Materials*

Another factor that affected the performance of these centres has the frequent interruption in the supply of materials viz. nutrition packages. The study of table shows that almost in all the centres supplementary nutrition could not be distributed between Oct. 91 to Jan. 92 and such instances occurred chronically. These interruptions broke the sequence as a result of which the distribution also suffered.

(v) *Lack of Coordination between Various Agencies*

The most disturbing part of the study has been the lack of coordination between various rural development agencies. The problem of rural development cannot be solved by discreet approaches as the problem in itself is multi dimensional. The drop in the level of immunization, pre schooling all vital components of the scheme largely suffered on account of lack of coordination between the departments such as health, jal nigam, sanitation etc.

(vi) *Lack of Awareness Among Rural Folks*

The low performance of these centres specially towards immunization and pre schooling has also been on account of low level of public awareness, which has also severely limited the scope of the scheme and since these centres do not have adequate staff and good inter departmental nexus consequently their performance suffers.

## Suggestions

In order to make these centres more meaningful one, it is recommended that besides equipping them with minimum basic facilities, like that of safe drinking water and toilets, it is equally important to provide these centres with full-fledged staff. Efforts should also be made to make all the centres fully operational as sub-optimal operation also affects the performance.

The regular supply of material to these centres be maintained or atleast improved. Provision for storing adequate stock in these centres be made so that even if the supply gets interrupted, the distribution aspects is taken care of.

The lack of cooperation between other departments/agencies has been of prime concern. The study of AW centres shows the extent to which these are suffering from under staffing syndrome, likewise it may be assumed that other departments and agencies too are facing the like wise problems. Under these circumstances, it may not be feasible to expect help from them and hence some other alternative avenue has to be explored whose services have either not been exploited or have been used very little and which also have the community support. As these rural areas also have many potential groups, voluntary organisations and our analysis reveals that so far their potential has not been utilised. It is, therefore, recommended that their support and services be used in the areas of creating awareness among the rural population about the on going schemes, disseminating knowledge about the advantages of educating females as well as immunization etc., bridging the hiatus between two or more department works etc.

Unless a massive campaign in these areas is taken up, the progress and the performance of AW centres will always remain susceptible.

## REFERENCES

1. NIPCCD (1992) : "National Evaluation of Integrated Child Development Services", New Delhi.
2. *Ibid* (1987) : "An Evaluation of Non-Formal Pre-School Education Component in Mangolpuri ICDS Block", New Delhi.
3. *Ibid* (1989) : "Status of Nutrition Component of ICDS", New Delhi.
4. *Ibid* (1992) : "Pre-School Education in ICDS : An Appraisal, New Delhi.
5. Govt. of India, Planning Commission, (1985) : "The Seventh Five Plan 1985-90' Vol.II," New Delhi.
6. Census of India (1981) : "District Census HandBook Series-22, Part XIII-A, Village & Town Directory, District Allahabad", New Delhi.

NINE

# RURAL DEVELOPMENT IN INDIA : A New Approach

A.D. SHARMA

For meaningfully analysing India's 'rural development paradigm', its problems, and perspectives, we have to clearly understand where we began in 1951, when the planned development experiment had set off. The premises, past and present, natural and human; social, political, demographic and economic; semantic and parametric have got to be clearly understood, if anything, to understand the future probabilities and to take relevant lessons.

Since 1951 'planning' has been the most major government technique for the country's development. Seven major plans and five one year plans have already been completed and the country is currently implementing its Eighth Five Year Plan (1992-97), in line with that policy.

Rural development has found place in our country's development effort in two ways. Firstly, there is a place assigned to rural development, importantly including agricultural and community development, in regular manner in development plans and, secondly, there are special specific efforts and measures undertaken by the government for the redress of backward rural folk.

## The Growth Effort

Taking just one indicator, the per capita per month expenditure, an average rural person was spending in one full month, in 1951, an amount of Rs. 20-00 (about 5 U.S. dollars at the then exchange rates). A twenty rupees of expenditure on one person in one month on his food, clothing, housing, health, education, in fact, on everything that one can think of, as worthwhile in life, and in living. In fact it was a colossus of abject poverty. The only assets were a firm determination to develop and a will to live.

And there it began. A planned effort. A journey, a pilgrimage to development. Government was committed to planning and the First Five Year Plan was launched in 1951, First, Second and Third Five Year Plans and then one-year plans followed by Fourth, Fifth, Sixth, Seventh and Eighth Five Year Plans with Annual Plans. In fact, 42 years of planning have been completed.[1a]

An enormous effort has been extended during planning for upliftment of the country (as also the upliftment of the rural part of the country).

## Multi-dimensions of the Problem

There can be a macro-picture. There can be a micro approach. There can be measures in general, encompassing the whole people, or at least most of the people, worst-affected. We can talk generally of the infrastructure, of the provision of capital, of banking facility, of better markets, of demand and of supply. And yet everything generalised may not be enough though it may be necessary.

There are, in fact, individuals who constitute the society. There are individuals who constitute groups and subgroups. These groups constitute the society. There are agriculturists. There are farmers and absentee agriculturists. The farmers cultivate their own land and non-cultivating farmers take their share from someone who cultivates their land. There are small farmers and big farmers. Even the small farmers can fall into numerous, very different and distinct categories. There are landless labourers who do farming. There are labourers who do other jobs like house repairs and the rest. There are also artisans and many other folk who might find some useful function in the village society.

When we are talking of rural development we are actually talking of development of this heterogeneous lot whose interests may not be similar or even collateral and who may not benefit from the same schemes and sometimes one and the same scheme may go in favour of some and quite clearly against the others. And still things have to be done, schemes have to be implemented and the society (the rural here in particular) has to develop.

It has to be painfully admitted that about half of the rural population is below the poverty line and it is really gruesome that the below-poverty-line chunk has not decreased atleast in absolute numbers over the years, over the whole period of planning.

The people above the poverty line too are not very well off barring a precious few, so-called *Kulaks*.

Thus, in fact, everybody in the rural populace has to be helped, has to develop, nationally, regionally, even individually, in a macro way and also in a micro way.

We are aware that this whole lot is characterised by a striking heterogeneity which fact we can ill-afford to ignore. Most people are engaged in agriculture but those engaged in agriculture too are extremely divergent in characteristics and there too no uniform schemes may be really adequate.

We therefore, have to settle that there would be macro-schemes like those affecting agricultural development but there also have got to be, as importantly, schemes to help specific weaker groups who have not benefited from the agricultural development schemes.

The rural scenario consists of farmers, agricultural labourers, functional workers and others.

Some of the farmers own land but there are others who do not own land. The land holdings of the farmers are of large, medium, small and marginal size. Most of the farmers not owning land are share croppers, those who work on land of absentee land owners or land owners who also work with these farmers. Then, there are agricultural labourers some of whom are even bonded labourers.

The functional workers in the rural setting are carpenters, iron-smiths, barbers, washermen, sweepers and others most of whom work for the rural community and work for very poor rewards.

In any case what we can read into the situation, obtaining in the Indian rurality, is that the measures envisaged for rural reconstruction have to include :

(i) Measures to develop agriculture;
(ii) Measures for relief for those who have inadequate land-holdings or no holdings and are still engaged in farming (but are not just labourers);
(iii) Measures to help agricultural labourers who are landless;

and

(iv) Measures to alleviate the wanting conditions of those who are not engaged in agricultural trades.

All this can be settled by taking following measures :

(i) Agricultural development;
(ii) Development of small, cottage and rural industries;
(iii) Development of Infrastructure generally and particularly; and
(iv) Finding employment venues for those who have no sources of livelihood of their own.

In India all these measures have been on the list. And yet the amount of development on record is much less than what was desired. The achievements are no mean but more was required, desired, promised and even targetted.

We repeat, all, that was desired, did not happen, could not be achieved

But we would also suggest that, on the whole, the approach has not been away from satisfactory.

There have been macro-plans for developing agriculture, for developing infrastructure generally and particularly. There have also been target-groups approaches and schemes for weaker sections.

But, we repeat once again, we have surely failed. We have failed to develop agriculture adequately. We have failed to develop other venues of employment to alleviate poverty. And also we have failed in bringing about human development.

**Errors and Redress and a New Approach**

India tried for development, socio-economic, of the rural masses as of the whole population in many ways, in almost all known ways, known to formal economics, a multi-channel exercise indeed.

For rural upliftment agricultural development was tried. Rural industries were encouraged and assisted. Infra-structure was improved.

And yet the results achieved were not of a desired level. Agriculture and rural industries all improved but did not improve adequately.

There are specific causes of shortcomings, causes answering shortfall in agricultural development, causes answering the sluggish picking up of rural industries.

But, then, there seems to be causes also more general, more spectrum, more penumberic, which have permitted nothing to come out well. These causes have to be thoroughly diagnosed and removed beyond doubt.

## Causes Oft-Pointed out and Oft-Lobbied

### (a) *Causes of Wanting Agricultural Development*[1b&2]

(1) Majority of holdings, uneconomic.
(2) Inadequate arrangement of rural credit.
(3) Undependable and inadequate irrigation facilities.
(4) Inadequate marketing facilities.
(5) Pricing not fair.
(6) New technologies have not percolated.
(7) Less powerful farmers have not benefited from facilities offered.
(8) Majority of farmers are not yet aroused to advance.

### (b) *Rural Industries have not picked up well*[3]

(1) Most rural folk are not aroused to advance.
(2) Very inadequate technical knowledge.
(3) Inadequate credit facilities.
(4) Inadequate marketing Facilities.

### (c) *The Infrastructure*

The infrastructure has not been able to change adequately and also the weaker sections have not been able to take advantage in an ostensible manner.

There is no gain saying the fact that the above mentioned causes and considerations are important. Definite action has to be taken and ought to be taken in these regards if rural development has to be made a reality.

And yet that would not be all. That would not make the rural economy bouncing. That would not make Indian rural economy self-sustaining, self-generating and self-propelling. That would certainly not transform India's average rural folk, living a religiously self-contained life, into an economic, modernly economic-man.

Rural India has a specific, a very specific milieu, as any society can and do have one, of its own. It has a definite and specific past, a history, a culture, a temper, an approach, and a mode of interaction to the external stimulii. All that has to be understood. And it is only with a full and clear understanding of all that, that, a rewarding action can be taken.

There is a peculiar built up of an average Indian rural folk. He is traditional. He is superstitious. He is other worldly. He is suspicious of all that government does. He is unchanging and he has very little acceptance for new ideas and innovations.

Depending upon the above analysis and upon the firm knowledge of the stark reality, we propose:

## An Extension Demonstration Approach of India's Rural Development[4]

### *Extension Work*

There has got to be a dedicated extension work, extending knowledge of desirability, techniques, processes and all possible details involved in the scheme of development.

### *Demonstration Venues*[5]

All development schemes have to be clearly demonstrated in his vicinity, preferably, in his village unit itself.

There should be demonstration centres where work is kept actually going on, upon the suggested schemes.

There have got to be demonstration agricultural farms actually running clearly on suggested improved lines following the suggested better techniques.

There have got to be demonstration centres for all work suggested, the suggested rural industries and the like.

These 'extension demonstration' units have to be established in all village units either by government functionaries or by the private working units, have to be commissioned for the purpose charged with the responsibility of imparting detailed knowledge to everyone concerned in the village system.

The facilities too, like credit, like inputs, have to be extended in the style of an 'extension' project and not in formal, official, impersonal and bureaucratic manner hitherto being followed.

## A Composite Development Planning[6]

As earlier pointed out, a composite approach composed of macro level planning of infrastructure and dominant rural industries, agriculture and the like along with target group development projects have got to function in an 'Extension Demonstration' style to really clinch results and to transform the simple rural folk gradually into a modernly economic man.

Ultimately the intellectual leadership, socio-economic leadership and political leadership have to set the path and schedule the process suggested as under:

(i) Extension Demonstration work, as an inspiration, a motivation and guidance;
(ii) The rural man be made (by being educated, enlivened, inspired) capable of being involved or capable of taking up the role of initiator himself;
(iii) Involvement then becomes established for the rural man;
(iv) He is then made to do better and better than what he was doing already;
(v) The technique, then, is upgraded and more resources are made available to him;
(vi) Cottage/rural/small scale industries are further upgraded and agricultural techniques are further modernised; and
(vii) Infrastructural and structural, moving up the ladder, goes side by side along with other developmental endeavour.

It has to be recognised that there is dearth of the necessary wherewithal and there is as well the dearth of that urge, that economic mentality, that approach to take advantage of the means, howsoever scarce. Material resources are absolutely called for but material resources alone would not ignite the propellers. The propulsion has to be set on. The man has to be inspired into the proper urge. Only an *Extension Demonstration approach* would do it. Then only, the economic man in this rural being would rise and, gathering whatever means has been made available and accessible and whatever technique has been laid bare, he would march and advance on the road to socio-economic development.

**REFERENCES**


1(a) Eighth Five Year Plan, pp. 27-56.

1(b) Economic Survey, 1992-93, Tables 543 to 549.

2. Dandekar, V.M. (1992) : *IASS*, Vol. 10, No. 3 p. 180.
3. Myrdal, Gunnar, *Asian Drama*, Vol. II, pp. 1207-1220, .
4. Dantwala, M.L. (Ed.) (1986) : *Proceedings*, Asian Seminar on Rural Development, IIM, Ahmedabad.
5. Rau, S.K. (Ed.) : *Rural Development in India*, NIRD, Hyderabad, pp. 1-35.
6. Bhagwati, Jagdish : *Economics of Underdeveloped Countries*, p. 147.

TEN

# THE DYNAMICS OF URBANISATION IN AVADH REGION OF UTTAR PRADESH

RAJ MANI TRIPATHI

Urbanisation is an important feature of the human evolution. Though the cities appeared about five thousand years ago, they were small in size and were surrounded by rural societies and agricultural fields. But now-a-days, all over the world large urban centres have sprung up and urbanisation has become a universal phenomenon and a greater part of population in the developed countries reside in cities.[1] Now urbanisation is being considered as a symbol of development. The country which is more urbanised is being regarded as a more developed nation.[2] With the growing impact of modernisation and changing proximate of the human society, urbanisation is being accepted as a way of life and it has become the essential part of the growth as well as an important index of material progress and prosperity of the society.

The present study attempts to bring out the salient features of dynamics of urbanisation in the Avadh Region of Uttar Pradesh. The data used for the purpose are mainly taken from the Census of India, 1981.[3]

## The Study Region

The Avadh Region covers a total area of 62,398 km.$^2$ It comprises of Lucknow and Faizabad divisions and extends over twelve districts of Uttar Pradesh (Fig. 10.1). Geographically it constitutes a part of the Upper Ganga Valley which is homogeneous in structure and relief. Except a few marginal variations in relief particularly in the *Khadar* region, it is characterised by plain topography. It extends over 440 km. from north-west to south-east and 272 km. from north to south. It has central

FIG. 10.1 : Avadh Region, Administrative Set-Up, 1981.

location in the context of the Ganga Valley. The Siwalik ranges constitute the northern boundary while the southern boundary is demarcated by the Ganga. The western boundary is formed by the Ram Ganga and the eastern boundary by the Gandak.

The Avadh region is regarded as the most fertile and densely populated alluvial tract of the Ganga plain. The region is rich in its history and possesses long unbroken chain of cultural heritage. Now the Avadh region can be identified as a cultural region based on the language of Avadh i.e. *Avadhi* which is spoken in Faizabad, Barabanki, Gonda, Sultanpur, Rae Bareli, Unnao, Lucknow, Hardoi, Sitapur and Kheri districts.

**Meaning of Urbanisation**

The term 'urban has acquired much wider connotation in India now than ever before. In the context of planning and development at the national, regional and local levels, reference is made to various economic and social problems connected with the urbanisation process and urban growth.

Urbanisation, as a process, involves the multiplication as well as the increase of the size of individual concentration.[4] Urbanisation in the demographic sense, is an increase in the proportion of the urban population (U) to the total population (T) over a period of time. As long as U/T increases there is urbanisation.[5]

Thus, it is quite evident that not a single but a combined set of socio-economic and demographic factors should be used for measuring the process of urbanisation in a region. Mitchell refers to urbanisation as being the process of becoming urban, moving to cities, changing from agricultural to other pursuits common to cities and corresponding changes in behaviour patterns.[6]

However, by Indian as well as western scholars, the increase in urban population is generally recognised as an important index of measuring urbanisation in any region. This increase or growth of urban population may be the result of natural growth[7] (the births over deaths) or increase in number of urban centres (either by origin of new urban centres or by rural urbanisation), or migration of people from rural to urban areas.[8]

In Avadh region as in the other developing countries, the natural growth in urban population is far behind the other processes of urbanisation. Formation of new urban centres, the conversion of villages into urban centres as well as migration of people from rural to urban areas are the basic tenets of urbanisation. Moreover, a number of villages were considered as urban centres in every successive census except in 1961 when 36 urban centres of the region were de-classified from the urban group. At the same time unemployed and employed persons with lower income in agricultural activities in rural areas were pushed towards urban centres in search of their livelihood and to earn higher income. Many urban facilities like higher education, technical and professional training, medical facilities, sanitation and employment opportunities etc. are also pulling rural people to adopt towns. Thus, the push and pull mechanism was mainly responsible for urban growth in addition to the natural growth of existing urban centres.

It would not be out of place to cite Prakasha Rao[9] who had studied closely the three distinct processes of urbanisation in India viz. (i) the metropolitanisation, (ii) the Commercialisation or intermediate urbanisation, and (iii) the rural urbanisation or subsistence urbanisation. By the process of metropolitanisation the large cities are emerging into metropolitan areas because of heavy migration of people from rural as well as from small and medium size urban centres. In the commercialisation or intermediate urbanisation, small urban centres are entering into medium and large size-urban centres and cities. The third process — rural urbanisation means the formation of new urban centres either by natural growth of villages or by administrative and political decisions.

In Avadh region only the last two processes are responsible for the present state of urbanisation. There is not even a single metropolitan centre developed so far in this less urbanised region. The rural urbanisation has been playing a vital role in the social transformation of the region.

## Trends of Urbanisation

In the least industrialised, agriculturally dominated and economically backward Avadh region, the process of urbanisation had very slow since the beginning of this century.[10] It is quite evident from Table 10.1 that in 1901 only 7.35 per cent of total population of the region was residing in urban centres but it was only 6.71 per cent in 1911 due to higher death rate in urban areas because of various epedimic diseases. Again it rose to 6.72 and 7.23 per cent in 1921 and 1931 respectively. In 1941 its 8.12 per cent population and had become urban and it was for the first time that after a gap of forty years (1901-41), the urban percentage crossed the level of 1901 (7.35 per cent).

However, urban population was recorded as 8.74, 8.41, 9.10 and 11.96 per cent in the successive years of 1951, 1961, 1971 and 1981 respectively.

Table 10.2 shows that total urban population in Avadh region was 9.39 lakhs in 1901 which declined by 10.23 per cent during the first decade of the twentieth century and thus remained only 8.43 lakhs in 1911. However, the urbanisation did not get a push upto third decade as only 1.53 per cent growth was recorded during thirty years (1901-31). But thereafter, urbanisation proceeded with faster rates and as result, during the last five decades (1931-81), urban centres experienced 230.45 per cent increase in their population. Thus, in 1941, 1951, 1961, 1971 and 1981 urban population of the region had reached 11.46, 13.57, 14.80, 18.65 and 30.56 lakhs. In this way, during the last 80 years, Avadh region experienced 225.37 per cent growth in its urban population, while Uttar Pradesh recorded 269.14 per cent during the same period.[11]

## Class-wise Growth of Urban Centres

For the analysis of class-wise growth of urban centres, the six categories of urban centres are used by the Census of India.[12] The Indian Census had adopted the population size as the main basis for classifying the urban centres (Fig. 10.2). According to it, all the urban settlements are graded into six classes[13] (Census of India, 1981), which differ widely in their population size and characteristics, and are recognised separately on the basis of their status, such as Urban Agglomeration (UA), Municipal Corporation (MC), Municipal Board (MB), Cantonment (Cantt.), Town Area (TA), and Notified Area (NA). Table 10.1 provides the distribution of all such centres of the region among six classes and compares the number of urban centres of each class and their population with each of the other classes on a time scale.

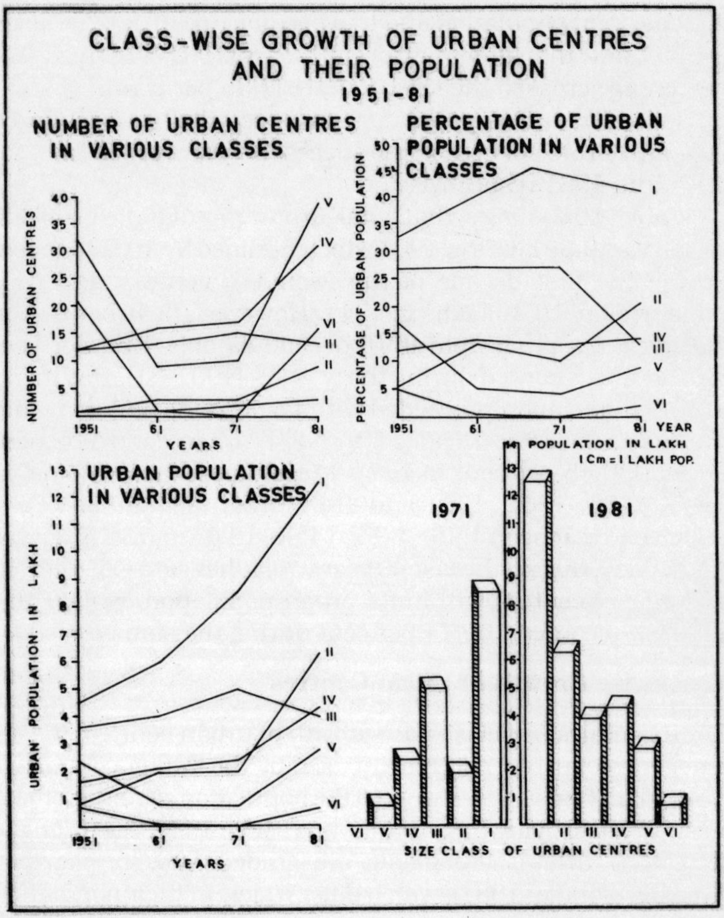


FIG. 10.2 : Class-Wise Growth of Urban Centres and their Population, 1951-81

TABLE 10.1 : Number and Population of Urban Centres (1981) and Changing Ratio of Urban Population to Total Population since 1901

| District | Total Popul-ation (in Lakhs) | No. of urban centres (1981) | Urban Population in per cent | | | | | | | | |
|---|---|---|---|---|---|---|---|---|---|---|---|
| | | | 1901 | 1911 | 1921 | 1931 | 1941 | 1951 | 1961 | 1971 | 1981 |
| Kheri | 19.53 | 9 | 3.71 | 3.00 | 3.81 | 4.83 | 5.36 | 7.30 | 5.53 | 6.21 | 9.60 |
| Sitapur | 23.37 | 10 | 6.67 | 6.54 | 7.61 | 6.27 | 6.68 | 7.52 | 7.63 | 7.54 | 10.29 |
| Hardoi | 22.75 | 13 | 9.35 | 7.64 | 3.97 | 8.70 | 9.45 | 9.01 | 7.26 | 7.90 | 11.06 |
| Unnao | 18.23 | 18 | 6.96 | 5.05 | 4.50 | 5.00 | 5.48 | 5.30 | 2.43 | 2.57 | 11.87 |
| Rae Bareli | 18.87 | 7 | 3.81 | 3.99 | 3.98 | 4.18 | 4.29 | 4.36 | 3.03 | 3.40 | 7.37 |
| Lucknow | 20.15 | 8 | 36.89 | 36.01 | 36.31 | 38.07 | 43.77 | 46.14 | 49.55 | 50.90 | 52.60 |
| Baharaich | 22.16 | 5 | 4.18 | 4.13 | 2.85 | 4.67 | 4.90 | 5.33 | 5.31 | 5.93 | 7.05 |
| Gonda | 28.35 | 11 | 4.26 | 3.54 | 3.67 | 4.26 | 5.67 | 4.88 | 4.88 | 5.65 | 7.32 |
| Barabanki | 19.92 | 12 | 5.74 | 5.41 | 5.56 | 6.18 | 6.71 | 6.59 | 4.97 | 5.76 | 8.93 |
| Faizabad | 23.83 | 7 | 10.24 | 8.25 | 7.96 | 9.01 | 7.64 | 9.26 | 8.68 | 9.56 | 10.96 |
| Sultanpur | 20.43 | 4 | 0.87 | 0.90 | 0.87 | 1.87 | 1.18 | 1.35 | 1.85 | 1.97 | 3.30 |
| Pratapgarh | 18.01 | 7 | 2.09 | 1.96 | 1.88 | 2.09 | 2.34 | 2.21 | 1.71 | 1.96 | 5.05 |
| Avadh Region | 255.58 | 111 | 7.35 | 6.71 | 6.72 | 7.23 | 8.12 | 8.74 | 8.41 | 9.10 | 11.96 |
| U.P | 1,108.62 | 655 | 11.08 | 11.19 | 10.57 | 11.19 | 12.41 | 13.64 | 12.85 | 14.02 | 17.95 |
| INDIA | 6,652.88 | 3,245 | 10.29 | 10.29 | 11.18 | 12.00 | 13.86 | 17.58 | 17.98 | 19.91 | 23.70 |

*Sources*: 1. Census of India, 1981, U.P. Part-II-A, General Population Tables
2. Census of India, 1981.

TABLE 10.2: Growth of Urban Population in Avadh Region and Uttar Prdesh (1901-1981)

| Year | Avadh Region | | | Uttar Pradesh | | | Per cent variation in urban Population of India |
|---|---|---|---|---|---|---|---|
| | Population in Lakhs | Variation in Population | Variation in Per cent | Population in Lakhs | Variation in Population | Variation in Per cent | |
| 1901 | 9.39 | – | – | 53.91 | – | – | – |
| 1911 | 8.43 | –0.96 | +12.23 | 49.07 | –4.84 | –8.98 | + 0.35 |
| 1921 | 9.18 | –0.25 | –3.0 | 49.36 | + 0.29 | + 0.59 | + 8.27 |
| 1931 | 9.25 | + 1.07 | +13.08 | 55.69 | + 6.33 | +12.82 | +19.12 |
| 1941 | 11.46 | + 2.21 | +23.89 | 70.16 | +14.47 | +25.98 | +31.97 |
| 1951 | 13.57 | + 2.11 | +18.41 | 86.25 | +16.09 | +22.93 | +41.42 |
| 1961 | 14.80 | + 1.23 | +9.06 | 94.80 | + 8.55 | + 9.91 | +26.41 |
| 1981 | 30.56 | +11.91 | +68.86 | 198.99 | +75.10 | +60.62 | +44.51 |

*Sources* :
1. Census of India, 1981, U.P. Part-II-A, General Population Tables
2. Census of India, 1981

Table 10.3 clearly shows the trends of growth of population and the rise in the numbers of various classes of urban centres. It may be pointed out that the changing trends are mainly due to the following four reasons : (i) the movement of urban centres of a particular class to a different class due to changes in the size of population; (ii) the elevation of formerly a rural area to an urban area, particularly as per census of 1981; (iii) the declassification in 1961 census of the swollen villages treated earlier as urban centres in 1951 census back to villages; and (iv) the amalgamation of a number of urban centres into corporation or Urban Agglomeration.

The number of urban centres in Avadh region were 79, 43, 47 and 111 in 1951, 1961, 1971 and 1981 respectively. The number of urban centres fell in 1961 because 36 of then were declassified from the urban group. Their number in each class has varied significantly from one census to the other and it has influenced much in recent decade the proportion of urban population of Avadh region. Remarkable decennial variations are noticed in the category of Class-I urban centres, which alone claimed 32.73, 40.23, 45.69 and 40.97 per cent of the total urban population of this region in 1951, 1961, 1971 and 1981 respectively. The large size urban centres (Lucknow, Faizabad and Sitapur) expanded much faster due to better industrial and commercial activities, public amenities and transport services. It is also noted that Lucknow, only one

TABLE 10.3 : Class-wise Distribution of Urban Centres and Urban Population in Avadh Region during 1951-81

| Year | I | | II | | III | | IV | | V | | VI | | TOTAL | |
|---|---|---|---|---|---|---|---|---|---|---|---|---|---|---|
| | No. | Pop. | No. | Pop. | No. | Pop. | No. | Pop. | No. | Pop. | No. | Pop. | No. | Pop. |
| 1951 | 1 | 32.73 | 1 | 5.64 | 12 | 26.80 | 12 | 12.10 | 32 | 17.38 | 21 | 5.35 | 79 | 100 |
| 1961 | 1 | 40.23 | 3 | 13.08 | 13 | 27.05 | 16 | 14.06 | 9 | 5.27 | 1 | 0.31 | 43 | 100 |
| 1971 | 2 | 45.69 | 3 | 10.37 | 15 | 26.99 | 17 | 12.93 | 10 | 4.02 | — | — | 47 | 100 |
| 1981 | 3 | 40.97 | 9 | 20.66 | 13 | 12.84 | 31 | 14.21 | 39 | 9.15 | 16 | 2.17 | 111 | 100 |

*Source* : Census of India, 1981, Uttar Pradesh, Part-II-B, Series-22, Primary Census, Abstract.

urban centre situated on the left bank of river Gomti, was under Class-I upto 1961, one additional urban centre of Faizabad joined Class-I in 1971. In 1981 census, Sitapur appeared as Class-I urban centre (Fig. 10.3). But the growth rate of Class-I cities was 46.93 per cent during 1971-81 as compared to 43.10 during 1961-71.

The Class-II urban centres have no definite trend as the number of such urban centres was only one in 1951 and three in 1961 as well as in 1971, but it suddenly rose to nine in 1981 and its growth rate was 221.58 per cent during 1971-81.

The Class-IV urban centres had a fluctuating trend as their number rose from 12 in 1951 to 16 in 1961, which further, increased from 17 in 1971 to 31 in 1981 and their percentage share in total urban population were 12.10, 14.06, 12.93 and 14.21 in 1951, 1961, 1971 and 1981 respectively. Sudden rise of population from 1971 to 1981 occurred due to the inclusion of 14 more new urban centres in this category. The variation is mainly due to the movement of urban centres in this category. The variation is mainly due to the movement of urban centres of a particular size-class to the other higher size-class.

As such in Class-V the number of urban centres were 32, 9, 10 and 39 (pop. 17.38, 5.27, 4.02, 9.15 per cent) in 1951, 1961, 1971 and 1981 respectively. Thus a remarkable change was recorded in 1961 and 1971. In these two Census i.e. 1961 and 1971 the same urban centres were declassified and excluded from urban group.

## Level of Urbanisation

In order to measure the level of urbanisation in various districts of the region at present and in the past the following criteria have been adopted according to the Census of India. The level of urbanisation is the ratio of urban population to total population (11.96 per cent). It is much less in comparison to Uttar Pradesh (17.95 per cent) and India (23.70 per cent). The study of level of urbanisation in the region is based on demographic data available at Tahṣil or sub-division level.[14] In Lucknow Tahsil the level of urbanisation was as high as 73.69 per cent in 1981, where as one tahsil named Musafirkhana (District Sultanpur) out of 47 tahsils of the region had not even a single urban centre and was purely rural in character. On the basis of their level of urbanisation, the 46 urbanised tahsils can be divided into four categories[15] : (i) Very Low urbanised area

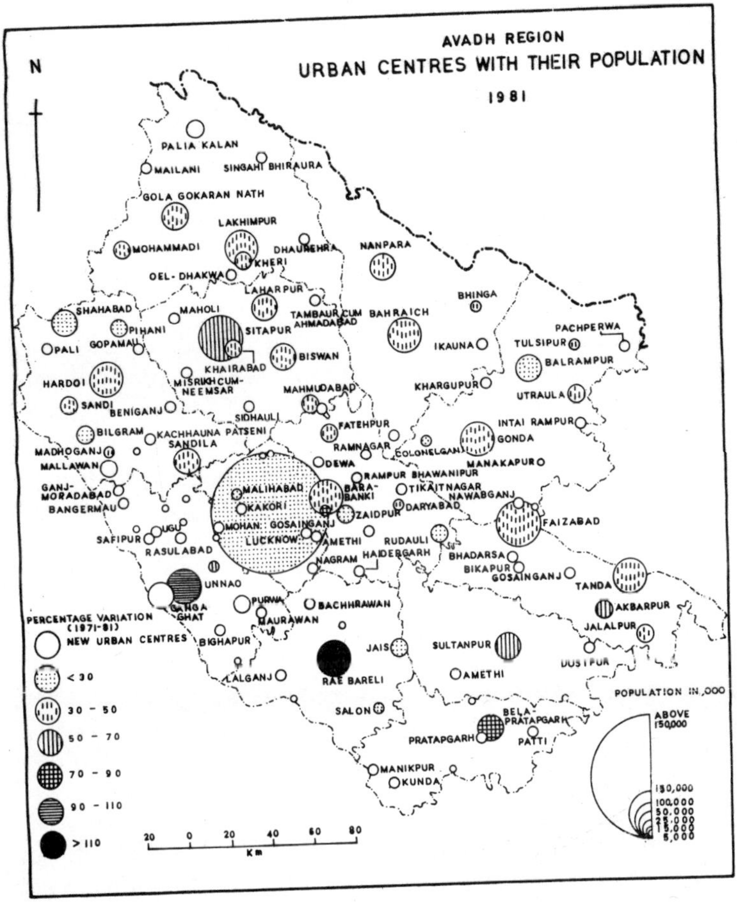


FIG. 10.3 : Avadh Region : Urban Centres with their Population, 1981

(below 5 per cent), (ii) Low urbanised area (5-15 per cent), (iii) Medium urbanised area (15-25 per cent), and (iv) High urbanised area (25 per cent and above (Fig. 10.4).

Eighteen tahsils are very low urbanised which are distributed all over the region. Tahsils of Sitapur, 22.34 per cent, Unnao 22.72, Rae Bareli 19.85, Bahraich 18.45 per cent, Nawabganj 18.44 and Amethi 19.19 per cent are medium urbanised areas of the region. There is one tahsil of Lucknow having 73.69 per cent of its population as urban which is about 9 times the regional average of urbanisation (8.25 per cent). It has been possible to the location of city Lucknow in this tahsil.

## Urban Density

This population density of a region indicates the relationship that exists between the number of inhabitants and the area of that region. Urban density which is also analysed on tahsil level, means the size of urban population per sq.km. area. It is also unevenly distributed through out the region ranging from 487 persons per sq.km. in Patti tahsil (Pratapgarh district) to 1,01,617 persons per sq.km. in Amethi tahsil (Sultanpur district). In this way all the urbanised tahsils can be grouped into six categories on the basis of urban density : (a) Area with very low urban density (below 2,000 persons/sq.km.), (b) Area with low urban density (2,000-4,000 persons/sq.km.), (c) Area with medium low urban density (4,000-6,000 persons/sq.km.), (d) Area with medium urban density (6,000-8,000 person/sq.km.), (e) Area with High urban density (8,000-10,000 persons/sq.km.), and (f) Area with very high urban density (above 10,000 persons/sq.km.)

Of all the 46 urbanised tahsils, 14 had very low urban density while 15 tahsils were included in the low category of urban density. Thus, 29 tahsils of the region had urban density below 4,000 person per sq.km., 13 tahsils are in the category of medium urban density. Two other tahsils are Salon, (9,701) and Nawabganj (8,332) are the high urban density. Only Amethi (1,01,617) and Nanpara (14,448) tahsils can be treated as area of very high urban density. (Fig. 5).

## Regional Pattern of Urbanisation

The region has 12 districts, all the districts of three region are

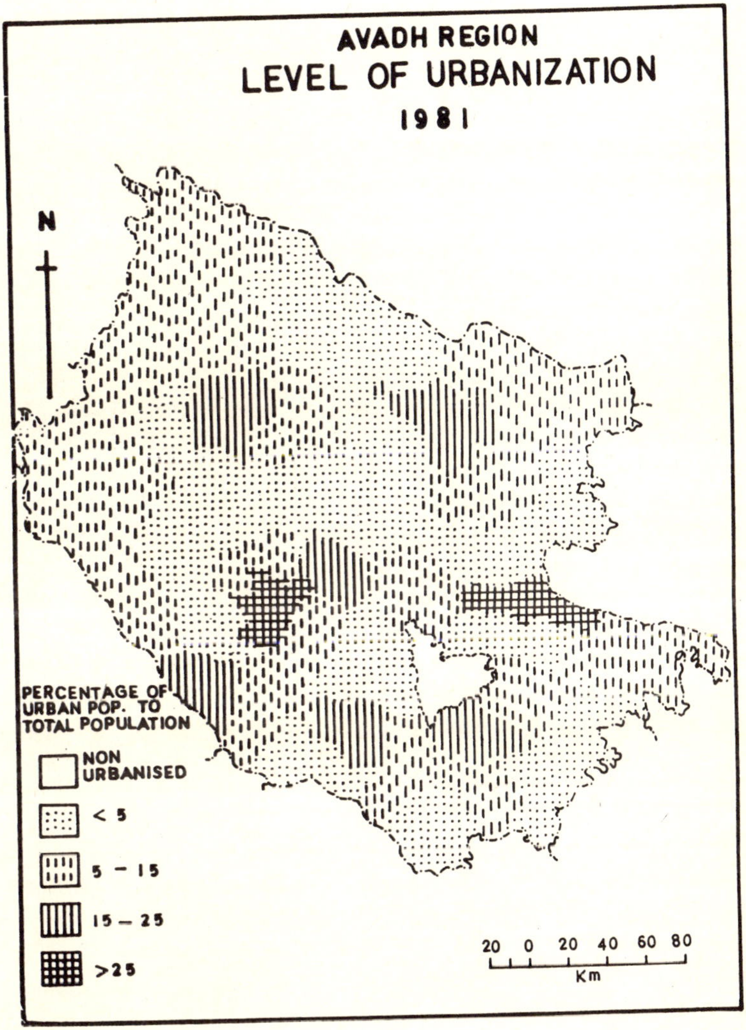


FIG. 10.4 : Avadh Region : Level of Urbanisation, 1981

divided into five sub-regions (Table 10.4) based on the location norms. The number of size of urban centres and growth rates as per six urban categories have been the main planks of the regional analysis.[16]

(a) *Northern Region*

It comprises 3 districts Kehri, Bahraich and Gonda. In this region 5.51 lakh population lives in urban area which is 7.87 per cent of its total population. The level of urbanisation in each district is far below the average urbanisation level of Avadh region. Out of 25 urban centres of the northern region, 5 are in Bahraich, 11 are in Gonda and 9 in Kheri. The class-wise distribution of the urban centres are 3, 4, 10, 6 and 2 in Class II, III, IV, V and VI respectively.

The Class-II towns of Bahraich (Pop. : 99,889), Gonda (70,847) and Lakhimpur (61,003) had average annual growth rates of 35.11, 34.53 and 39.43 per cent respectively during 1971-81. Mailani, Singahi, Bhiraura, Dhaurehra, Palia Kalan and Oel Dhakwa in Kheri; Katra, Kharagpur in Gonda got the change to become towns for the first time in 1981.

TABLE 10.4: Spatial Pattern of Urbanisation in Avadh Region (1981)

| Region | Number of Urban Centres | Urban Population in 000 | Urban Population in % | Per cent Variation 1971-81 | Per cent Variation 1901-81 | Level of urbanisation in % |
|---|---|---|---|---|---|---|
| 1. Northern | 25 | 551.12 | 18.04 | + 69.61 | 301.49 | 7.87 |
| 2. Eastern | 11 | 328.57 | 10.75 | + 51.76 | 144.02 | 7.42 |
| 3. Southern | 14 | 229.92 | 7.53 | + 278.15 | 413.93 | 6.53 |
| 4. Western | 31 | 1527.63 | 49.99 | + 51.58 | 230.16 | 24.99 |
| 5. Central | 30 | 418.46 | 13.69 | + 77.10 | 186.33 | 6.67 |
| TOTAL | 111 | 3055.71 | 100.00 | + 63.85 | 225.38 | 11.96 |

*Source*: Census of India, 1981, Uttar Pradesh, Part-II-B, General Population Tables.

(b) *Eastern Region*

The eastern districts of the region – Faizabad and Sultanpur make this sub-division having 3.28 lakh urban population. Itnhas second place in the level of urbanisation (7.42 per cent).

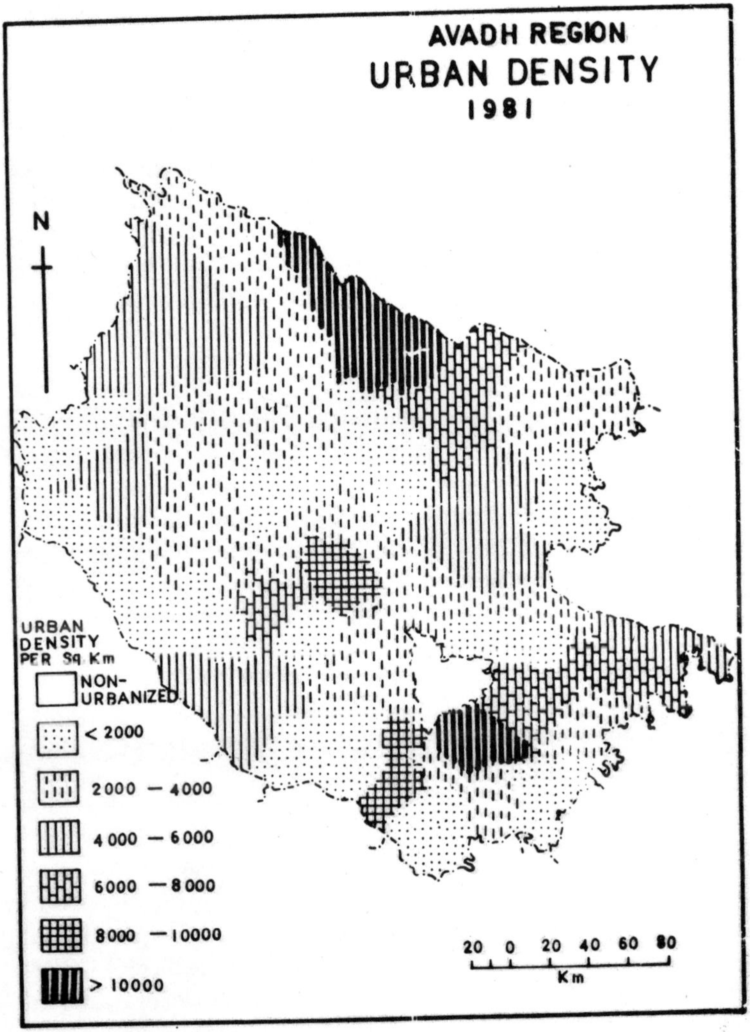


FIG. 10.5 : Avadh Region : Urban Density, 1981

in Faizabad and Sultanpur districts, the percentage of urban population was only 10.96 per cent and 3.30 per cent respectively. This region has 11 urban centres, 7 are in Faizabad and 4 in Sultanpur. The number of urban centres in Class-I, II, III, IV, V and VI are 1, 1, 1, 3, 4 and 1 respectively.

Faizabad (Pop.: 1,43,167) is the only Class-I urban centre in this Sub-region which had experienced 30.28 per cent average annual growth rate during 1971-81. In 1981 census, Bikapur and Bhadarsa (district Faizabad) and Amethi, Dostpur, Koeripur (District Sultanpur) had been recognised as new urban centres. Out of these 5 urban centres one is in Class-VI and other 4 are in Class-V.

(c) *Southern Region*

Rae Bareli and Pratapgarh districts are the representative of the southern sub-region having 2.29 lakhs urban population comprising 6.23 per cent of its total population in 1981. The number of urban centres are in all. Rae Bareli (89,697). Pratapgarh (49,932), are the Class-II and Class-III urban centres which experienced 131.39 and 78.91 per cent growth during 1971-81. This region has got the chance to have 11 urban centres (5 in Rae Bareli and six in Pratapgarh) for the first time in 1981. Out of 11 new urban centres are) 2, 5, 4 in Class-IV, V and VI respectively.

(d) *Western Region*

The district of Hardoi and Unnao constituting the western sub-region had 15.27 lakh urban population which was 24.99 per cent of their total population. Out of 31 urban centres of the region, 13 are located in Hardoi and 18 are in Unnao district.

The number of urban centres is recorded as 2, 4, 7, 11 and 7 in Class-II, III, IV, V and VI respectively. Hardoi (67,259) and Unnao (75,983) are the Class-II urban centres which experienced 44.21 and 98.91 per cent decade growth rate during 1971-81. The region has got the chance to have 13 urban centres (7 in Unnao and 6 in Hardoi) for the first time in 1981.

(e) *Central Region*

This sub-region has 3 districts namely, Lucknow, Barabanki

and Sitapur which are located in the central part of Avadh region. This sub-region has 4.18 lakh urban population and 6.67 per cent as level of urbanisation. The level of urbanisation of Lucknow District (52.60 per cent) is much higher than the average of Avadh region (11.96 per cent) or that of Uttar Pradesh (17.95 per cent).

## REFERENCES


1. Mukerji. A.B., Chandra, R.C and Bali, P.K. (1971) : "Urbanisation in the Districts Surrounding the Union Territory of Delhi, : 1951-61", *Man Power Journal*, 7(3), New Delhi, pp. 64-78.
2. Singh, L.R. (1985) : *Role of Small and Medium Towns in Regional Development : A Case Study of Uttar Pradesh.*
3. Census of India (1981), Uttar Pradesh, Part-II-B, Primary Census Abstract.
4. Sharma, O.P. : "Social Development of Urbanisation in India", *Indian Journal of Social Research*, Vo. XXXII, No. 2, p. 97.
5. Bose, A. (1973) : *Studies in India's Urbanisation*, Tata McGraw Hill Publishing Co., Bombay, p. 3.
6. Mitchell, J.C. Quoted in Gerald Breese (1969) : *Urbanisation in Newly Developing Countries*, Prentice Hall of India, New Delhi, p. 3.
7. Davis, Kingsley (1962) : "Urbanisation in India : Past and Future", in Roy Turner (ed.), *India's Urban Future*, Oxford University Press, Bombay, p. 1.
8. Maurya, S.D. (1988) : *Urban Environment Management : A Functional Study*, Chugh Publication, Allahabad, p. 37.
9. Prakasha Rao, V.L.S. (1973) : *The Process of Urbanisation*, Fulbright, New letter, March, New Delhi, pp. 10-14.
10. Singh, R.L. (1956) : The Trends of Urbanisation in Umland of Banaras, *NGJI*, 75, 83.
11. Lall, A. and R. Tirtha (1968) : India's Urbanisation, *Focus*, 19, 1-6.
12. In 1981 Census, the towns have been classified in the following six classes according to their population -

| | |
|---|---|
| Class-I | 100,000 and over |
| Class-II | 50,000 — 99,999 |
| Class-III | 20,000 — 49,999 |
| Class-IV | 10,000 — 19,999 |
| Class-V | 5,000 — 9,999 |
| Class-VI | Less than 5,000 |

13. *Ibid.*, 1981, Part II-B.
14. Mukerji, A.B. (1973) : 'Levels of Urbanisation in Uttar-Pradesh', *Geog. Rev. India*, 35, 31-43.
15. UNESCO (1956) : *Report on Urbanisation in Asia and Far East*, Bangkok.
16. Singh, U. (1970) : 'Urbanisation of Population—A Geographical Analysis', *Uttar Bharat Bhoogal Patrika*, Gorakhpur, Vol. 6, No. 1, p. 1.

ELEVEN

# SOME ASPECTS OF ENERGY USE IN U.P. HIMALAYAS

K.N. BHATT

Energy is the basic component of survival of all the life forms and activities. It is the most important factor for economic development and human welfare in a country. Levels of energy production and energy utilization in a nation are used as the indicators of prosperity in modern times. The pace of industrial growth or of all the other economic development activities rest on the adequate supply of energy. Adequate production of energy and its effective utilization has, therefore, been one of the most important endeavours of the planning process in our country. In spite of approximately one-third of our total plan outlays earmarked for the development of energy sector in Seventh and Eighth Five-Year Plans, there is an acute shortage of energy in all the sectors of our economy.

## Forms of Energy

There are various forms and sources of energy which are presently being used in our country. The main sources of primary commercial energy are coal, lignite, crude oil, natural gas, hydro-electric power and nuclear power. Industry, transport, household and agriculture, the four major sectors of our economy, consume about 51, 23, 14, and 10 per cent of total commercial energy produced, respectively. Besides the commercial energy, about 50 per cent of total energy requirement of the country is met by non-commercial sources namely wood, agricultural waste and animal dung. The entire household sector in rural areas and a large sector in urban areas depend on these sources of energy to fulfil their needs for cooking, heating and several other domestic requirements.

The main problems faced in the use of commercial fuels are

the scarcity of fossil fuels, their concentration in few areas, costly transportation, high costs of import and environmental pollution etc. These problems may be overcome, to some extent, by the use of non-conventional renewable sources of energy like solar, wind, tidal, bio-gas, bio-mass, mini and micro hydro-power projects, geo-thermal and hydrogen etc. These sources are very important in the context of rural development in India. The crux of the problem, thus, lies in finding alternative sources of energy to meet the growing demands of development and human welfare. This can be achieved only when we maintain a proper balance of locally available and socially acceptable alternative sources of energy. This calls for an intelligent management of the renewable and non-renewable, conventional and non-conventional and commercial and non-commercial sources of energy.

**The Present Paper**

The paper seeks to highlight the pattern of energy use and problems faced by the people of U.P. Himalayan region. What are the efforts made by the process of planning to ameliorate the problem of energy and how the people of the region have been benefited by these measures ? What alternative sources of energy are available in the region and how these resources can be utilized to benefit the local people ? Apart from answering these questions, an endeavour would also be made to analyze the basic social and economic issues in considering the alternative sources of energy for the hill region of Uttar Pradesh.

**Uttar Pradesh Himalayan Region**

The Uttar Pradesh Himalayan region, with a total geographical area of 51,125 sq. km.[1], extends over eight hill districts of Almora, Pithoragarh, Nainital, Garhwal, Chamoli, Tehri Garhwal, Dehra Dun and Uttarkashi. Altitude in the region varies from about 300 meters in the foothills to the highest snowbound mountain ranges like Nanda Devi, Kamet, Trishul, etc. crossing well over 7,500 meters. The maximum and minimum temperature ranges from about $30^0$ centigrade to (-) $5^0$ centigrade at different heights. The Ganga, the Yamuna, the Kali, the Dhauli, the Gori, the Ramganga, the Sarju, the Kosi, the Pinder, the Tons, the Mandakini etc. are the most important rivers of

Northern India, which originate from the U.P. Himalaya and flow through the foothills to the Gangetic plains. The entire region is mountainous with its undulating topography and terrain.

## Three Sectors of the Hill Economy

The population of U.P. hill districts has increased from 1.65 million in 1901 to 5.87 million in 1991[2] which equals to an increase of about 355 per cent. Above 80 per cent of the people live in rural areas who largely depend on agriculture, animal husbandry and forestry for their survival. These closely knit inter-dependent three sectors of hill economy, which even today remain geographically, socially, culturally and economically most suitable and fulfil almost all the requirements of the people since time immemorial. No development process can succeed without the proper development of these sectors of economy. Before dealing with the problem of energy, we must have some basic knowledge of the state of these sectors in the hill region of Uttar Pradesh which have obvious bearing on the energy problems of the people.

### *Agriculture*

Concentrated mainly in the outer Himalaya and low hills, the area under agriculture forms a very small proportion of the total area of the region. Presently the area under cultivation is around 13 per cent which, except in deep valleys, is of poor quality being shallow, poor textured, steep sloped and mostly rainfed. Only around one-fourth of the net area sown is irrigated. The land holdings are small in size which are scattered and fragmented. Except in the districts of Nainital and Dehra Dun which consist of large plains areas, in the rest of the hill districts the growth rate of agricultural production in general has remained either static or negative. The mechanization of agriculture is not feasible and therefore, all the agricultural operations are performed by human and animal power.

### *Forest*

Considered as the inexhaustible stock of forest wealth in U.P. Himalayas by Britishers when the region came under their administration, the entire area today stands at the verge of alarming depletion of forest resources. The forests in the hills fulfil the basic requirements of fuel, fodder, timber and several other household and agricultural needs. In the words of S.L. Shah[3], who has projected the demand and supply of forest produce for the year 2031 on the basis of present trends of consumption and pressure on forest, "that around 2031 A.D. the requirements of local people alone will exceed the total forest stock available which means that the carrying capacity of the forest will be over reached. Thus, at the ongoing rate of forest exploitation and population explosion an irreversible process will start in 2031 A.D." Treated as the biggest source of revenue earning, the degradation of forest, without any consideration for the needs of local people and tree species, was started by British administration and unfortunately the process still continues even after 46 years of independence. Recent satellite imageries show that the percentage of area under good quality forests has come down to around 25 as against the National Forestry Resolution, 1952 recommending 66 per cent of total geographical area under forest in the hills.

Native Oak and other broad leaf variety forests, which were found in abundance till the management of these forests remained in the hands of local people, are facing complete extinction. These tree species not only provide green fodder for animals, rich manure for agricultural fields, a variety of agricultural implements with their fine wood and fulfil a number of other household needs of the local people, but also were responsible for the underground water supply in the whole region for drinking as well as irrigation. With their maximum rain water retention ability, the Oak forests grow above an altitude of 5000 ft. and recharge the underground water only to flow out in the forms of beautiful natural springs in lower altitudes and deep valleys. However, with the introduction of exotic and commercial tree species and the wanton destruction of Oak forests, the natural system of water supply is nearing an end.

### *Animal Husbandry*

According to livestock census of Uttar Pradesh, the livestock population in the Hill Region has increased to 4.02 million in 1982 from 3.80 million in 1961.[4] With the degradation of grazing and pasture land and all type of forest lands, the availability of fodder and grass has reached its lowest levels. The main problem faced by the people of the region therefore, is how to feed such a large number of cattle ? In the absence of any alternative sources of fodder and grass, the first sickle falls on the fodder trees of whatever size or shape which are lopped badly to feed the hungry stallfed animals. In addition, cattle and goats roaming in forest and grass lands in acute fodder scarcity conditions eat away small upcoming saplings to further degrade these lands. Since animal power is an essential component of cultivation in this region, all the farm families keep a number of cattle and goat to perform several agricultural operations, manure their fields with cowdung and to fulfil their needs of milk and meat.

## Pattern of Energy Use in U.P. Himalayas

Undulating topography and terrain, widely varying climatic conditions, remoteness and inaccessibility of many places, variation in altitudes and very small and scattered plots of terraced land are some of the special characteristics of the himalayan region which makes the pattern of energy consumption quite different in comparison to the plains. Industry, transport, household and agriculture, the conventional four major energy consuming sectors of economy present a very different pattern of the use of energy in this region.

### *Industry*

In the race for industrial development, the region remains very backward due to the lack of basic infrastructural facilities, difficult geo-physical conditions of topography and terrain and neglect of the area by our planners. In the event of Chinese aggression in 1962 the problems of basic transport, communication and other infrastructural facilities came to surface and it was realized that the region is strategically very important from the point of view of our national defense as it shares international boundaries with China (Tibet) and Nepal. It is, therefore, only from the concern of national defence some development work started taking place in the region. With these developments a few modern industries particularly electronic and precision industries, have started coming up in the hills. This industrial development is still at its infancy and the power needs of these units is very small which can also be met easily if the hydro power potential of the region is harnessed properly through small hydro projects. Some traditional small and household industries that exist in the region are basically run on the basis of human power.

### *Transport*

As stated above, the region was connected to the rest of the nation through the network of roads after the Chinese aggression of 1962 particularly from the defense considerations. This network of roads cannot be expanded on an unlimited scale as the landscape of the region is very sensitive to such construction activities which bring along massive environmental destruction. It is, therefore, obvious that except for the small long distance road transport network which is run on petrol and diesel, all the activities in transportation are performed by human and animal power throughout the region where the modern roads are not in existence. In addition, energy needs of construction of roads, bridges, houses and other community services are also fulfilled by human and animal power.

### *Household Sector*

The household sector is the largest energy consuming sector in the U.P. Himalayas mainly for the purposes of cooking, heating, lighting and water heating. Almost entire energy requirements, of this sector, particularly in rural areas, are met by firewood which is gathered free from civil *soyam, panchayat* forests and reserved forests by the users themselves. The work of gathering firewood is that of women and children who spent whole day, walking over a distance of around 10 to 15 kms., to fetch a head load of wood. Excessive population pressure on forests, lopping of trees and overgrazing of pastures and forest lands, indiscriminate felling of trees, exploitative forest policy, extension of agricultural land to higher altitudes due to non-availability of land in deep valleys, mining, quarrying, road and house construction activities are some of the factors responsible for the large scale destruction of forests which is creating a dangerous situation of scarcity of fuelwood for the people of this region. Treated collectively as their own and culturally fitted into the life styles of the local people, forests were brought up and nurtured for generations in the U.P. Himalayas as a public property to provide, among other numerous benefits, an uninterrupted supply of free fuelwood. By creating reserved forests out of bonds for the local people, introducing price mechanism, policing and the so called modern day's forest management practices, we cannot preserve and protect our forests in the region. Fuel wood is considered as free good from the forests and even in the conditions of scarcity, it continues to be the most important source of energy presently and in future.

### *Agriculture*

As mentioned above, mechanization of agriculture in the hills is not possible and, therefore, all the energy requirements in this sector are fulfilled by animal or human power. Since natural springs and small streams, the perennial sources of potable water and irrigation, are drying up due to large scale deterioration of forests, lift irrigation system from rivers that flow in deep valleys is the need of the hour if agriculture is to be saved. It is only for the purpose of lift irrigation and drinking water schemes electricity is needed in agriculture. The solution to the problem also lies within the region if the vast potential of hydro power is utilized through mini hydro projects.

## Energy Planning and its Possible Potential

Conservation of land, water and forest resources with cooperation and participation of local people should be the primary objective of any energy planning in U.P. Himalayas. The region has vast potential of self reliance in energy with its internal sources if utilized in a scientific way keeping in view the cultural, locational and other specific requirements of the local people. This is not only necessary to preserve the physical wealth and maintain an ecological balance in the region but also very important for the well being of the people living in whole of the Gangetic plain of our country. Wastage of energy sources and excessive strain on some of the natural renewable resources without having any consideration to replenish them in a proper way would certainly have disastrous bearing on the economic, social and cultural well being of the people. Any source of energy that is socially acceptable, economically viable, environmentally sound, renewable and convenient in use would surely solve the problem of energy in the hills.

For the generations people of the region have been utilizing non-commercial sources of energy considering them as the free gift of nature. Efforts to switch over to commercial form of energy, therefore, are liable to be restricted. With technological innovation, education and participation of local people, efforts to rejuvenate the depleting renewable energy resources, particularly tree cover and pastures, of the region can initially be subsidized and gradually the system of energy supply would become sustainable and self reliant in the long run. How and in what ways the goal can be achieved ? To find an answer to the question, we will have to look into the prospects and potential of various forms of energy that are being used presently and could be used in future as alternative sources.

*Firewood*

Firewood is the most dependable and important source of energy supply in the household sector of hill economy. According to NCAER Survey, 1985 per capita annual household consumption of firewood in the hill regions of India is 294.43 kg.[5] Looking at the size of population in the study area, the volume of the total requirement works out to be large which goes beyond the carrying capacity of the existing forest stock of the region. There are many villages in the region where every stick of wood is collected and even the roots of trees are dug out to satisfy the need of the fuel for cooking and heating. As mentioned earlier, forests are being over-exploited not only for firewood but also for various other requirements of local public and to fill the coffers of the government through commercialisation. The situation is taking dangerous turns with ever increasing firewood demand of fast growing population and causing severe hardship to the people. Solutions to prevent such a situation can still be found if we act sincerely to achieve the following goals :

1. A massive afforestation drive is needed with the cooperation of local people without any further delay. Multipurpose, mixed variety of plants should be planted. Every patch of land that can be made available for plantations should be utilized not only to provide fuelwood, fodder and other day to day consumption needs of the people but also to save soil, water, land system and prevent the

problem of overall ecological imbalance which the region is presently facing as a result of large scale felling of trees. Indigenous tree species would only succeed in maintaining the fragile ecological balance in Himalayas and therefore, an urgent need of the hour is to plant Oak forest between the altitudes of 5000 ft. to 7000 ft. wherever it is possible. Fast growing exotic trees species can be tried to solve short-term problems, not for the long-run.

2. Whereas the local people are facing severe hardships of fuelwood, fodder and timber, forest department through forest corporation exports not only a large quantity of commercial timber but also takes away even the dried small branches of wood. It is this attitude of highhandedness and injustice by the department, people are compelled to treat government forests as their enemy. In these circumstances, government should give top prio-rity to satisfy local requirements, take people into confidence to plant trees and protect forests. Biggest challenge today is not to serve the petty commercial interests but to restore the very existence of the Himalaya which is at stake.
3. Firewood stalls should be opened up in the villages from where, in exchange of plantation work by women and children through various rural development schemes launched in lean seasons, firewood can be provided to the people. These plantation schemes can be worked out for individual farm lands, grass lands, *gram samaj, civil soyam, panchayat* forests and even degraded sites of reserved forests with an assured right of the people over the planted trees. By making these provisions, whereas, the short-term crisis of firewood can be solved by wood stalls, the planted trees when matured would take care of the growing demand in the long-run.
4. Traditional method of cooking and water heating in open *chulhas* waste around 90 to 95 per cent of the total potential energy of firewood which can be saved by the use of efficient cooking devices. People can be cautioned and made aware of the wastage through the use of government media and ground level extension network to change their traditional habits gradually and switch over to the use of fuel efficient *chulhas*. Even an efficiency level of 30 to 40 per cent is achieved, a large amount of dwindling firewood reserves can be saved. While design-

ing these devices social habits, customs, beliefs, whether conditions, food habits etc. must be studied in detail to make the programme socially acceptable and successful.

**Bio-gas and Bio-mass**

Sufficient organic waste materials are available in the hill areas of U.P. from agriculture, forests and livestock population which can be successfully converted into efficient forms of energy by using bio-gas plants, gasifiers, briquetting fuel plants etc. The use of bio-gas and bio-mass technology converts organic matter into methane and carbon-dioxide, the highly inflammable gasses used as a source of energy for cooking, lighting, and heating. The remaining decomposed organic matter from the plant with added nutrients can also be used as manure in agricultural fields. Small twigs, bushes, agro-wastes and particularly pine needles which are available in abundance in chir-pine forests, can also be converted into smokeless, efficiently burning briquettes in briquetting plants. The development of these systems of bio-energy for household consumption would reduce the excessive pressure on forests for firewood, lessen the burden of extra work on women and children who travel 10 to 15 kms. everyday in the process of fetching fuelwood and improve the prospects of ecological stability.

Although great potential for the development of bio-gas and bio-mass exist in the area, past experiences, however, prove that bio-gas and bio-mass plants are neither popular in this region nor the government have made serious efforts to popularize and develop these resources properly. The main reasons behind the discouraging results of these plants are reported to be, at first, low and varying atmospheric temperature in the hills that reduces the generation of gas in the plant. Secondly, water, which is required in equal amount to decompose the organic materials in plants, is not sufficiently available in most of the villages in the hills. In these villages collection of water from distant places even for drinking and other important domestic uses is a very troublesome and time consuming process. Thirdly, since people of the region collect firewood free of cost for cooking, water and space heating etc., high investments on the establishment of a gas plant appears to them as an uneconomic preposition. Fourth, with the average size of 5 to 6 small cattle heads per hill family, where animals go for grazing during day time due to the non-availability of fodder for stall feeding and their droppings are left out, the recovery of cattle dung for bio-gas plant remains inadequate. Therefore, for the average small size poor families it is not feasible to sustain an uninterrupted production of gas.

In spite of the difficulties mentioned above the great potential of organic waste material based system of energy that is available in the hills can be exploited for the welfare of the people and overall ecological and environmental stability of the region. The following efforts, therefore, could be made to revitalize the process of tapping these energy sources.

1. Through vigorous research and development efforts, making of a technological breakthrough is necessary for the proper utilization and exploitation of these waste bio-material resources of the region. Reduction in the cost of the presently used gas plants and their installation charges and the improvements in the design and efficiency are needed if the programme is to succeed. Several bio-mass materials should be tested to find their suitability and convenience for the production of gasses and other type of energy useful for household consumption. To cope with the problem of low temperature in higher altitudes, particularly above 3000 ft., solar canopy to heat the plant could be provided.
2. Most of the forests presently existing in the U.P. hills are that of *Chir*. Needle like leaves of *Chir* are known as pine-needles which fall down in sufficient quantity on the ground when dried. These pine needles dangerously prevent any kind of under growth vegetation and make the ground much slippery for animals, humans and even for the rain water that slides down to the narrow gorges in the absence of any ground level vegetation and degraded soil without being recharged under ground. To make use of the pine-needles, which presently are proving very harmful, government can select suitable sites and establish briquetting plants. The briquetted pine-needles, "by a process of extrusion and compaction can be converted into highly efficient briquettes which burn smokelessly".[6]

## Mini and Micro Hydro Power

All the major rivers of Northern India originate from U.P. hills with a beautiful system of thousands of sub-rivers and streams joining the main channels in the area. The natural system of main and sub-rivers, which flow full of water throughout the year in whole of the region, presents a great potential for mini- and micro-hydro power. Presently for lighting purposes, kerosene oil and highly inflammable parts of *Chir* and *Deodar* wood, locally known as *Dyar*, are being burnt in household sector. To save these scarce resources, a massive electrification drive in the villages can be started by exploiting the vast potential of water resources through micro- and mini-hydro projects with full cooperation and management of local people. An example of *Pan Chakkis* would suffice here to see that how the water power is traditionally being successfully exploited for centuries in the region. These *Pan Chakkis* are run to grind flour by throwing water directly into wooden turbines with high force without converting it into the power of electricity. Big dams to exploit hydro power prove to be a curse in this area, as the region is highly prone to large scale environmental destruction.

The main argument given against the mini and micro hydro projects is the high cost of electricity generation per unit. The cost of delivered power, however, is also minimized when we consider the relatively short distances of power delivery and minimum losses on the transmission and distribution from these power projects in comparison to large units. The cost incurred by big dams in terms of men, material and over all irreparable ecological devastation are so large that goes beyond our imagination. It is therefore, not only the accountable costs that should be considered but also the unaccountable ecological costs that we have to pay as a result of such schemes. The amount of Rs. 750 crores, that is claimed to be being spent in the construction of Tehri Dam, according to Sri Sunder Lal Bahuguna[7], we could have established around 2000 small hydro projects in the hills. By doing so, we would have neither committed such big scale extravagance, bribery and useless works, nor displaced large number of people and killed the whole river system. The greenery of the hills would have been restored, and in this way the expenditure on small hydro projects would have proved as an expenditure on capital formation. The author has given the example of highly successful and people's participatory programme of mini and micro hydro power projects in Chine, where upto 1991 around 60,000 of such units were in operation with an installed capacity of

13,850 MW employing 5,00,000 persons. Likewise the small irrigation canals, *Van Panchayats* and *Pan Chakkis*, which were successfully managed by the people of the region, we will have to adopt the principles of self-construction, self-management and self-consumption for the success of small hydro projects in the hills. In brief, for a successful programme of the development of small hydro projects, an environmentally pollution free renewable source of energy, we must take the following initiatives.

1. Clusters of adjoining villages should be identified and suitably selected to establish small hydro projects with full cooperation of local residents in construction, management and maintenance of these units. Initially all concessions and finances for the construction and electric connections should be provided by the government and local people can contribute as *shramdan*. After the electrification and fulfilling the needs of all the villages of the cluster, additional power, if produced may be diverted to the central grid established for this purpose from where power can be sold to other areas and industries to earn revenue for the long-term maintenance and management of these units.
2. Small household industries run on the basis of electric power, local skills and raw material should be started for the greater diversification of economic activities in the hills. The use of electric power can also be made for lift irrigation and drinking water schemes. This will not only increase many times agricultural and fruit production but also remove severe hardships faced by the people in the collection of potable water from distant places. This will ultimately help to bring alround development of the people in the hill region.

### Kerosene Oil and LPG

Kerosene oil is used by the rural households in hill areas for lighting purposes. It is supplied through public distribution system at various co-operatives and licensed shops. Being a priced commodity from the market, people use it for the limited purpose even in lighting as a supplementary to their own traditional lighting system of *Dyar* wood from *Chir* and *Deodar* trees. The scope for increasing its use is therefore, very limited. Efforts must be made to replace these primitive systems of lighting by a suitable policy of hundred per cent electrification of villages through the decentralized system of mini and micro hydro power projects.

The distribution of LPG, which had already been introduced in the area, may be increased in urban centres to save scarce firewood resources. In rural areas, neither the people would be interested to bear any monetary cost for fuel as it is considered free, nor it is possible to maintain a continuous supply of gas cylinders in most of the villages which are remote and inaccessible.

**Solar and Wind Energy**

Solar power, the inexhaustible renewable source of energy, that is available to the earth surpasses thousands of times of our total present day requirements. It is proved that the sun's rays can be used to generate electricity. Unfortunately, no convenient, cheap and feasible technology has however, been found till today to exploit the additional source of power being wasted, for the welfare of mankind. Presently available costly forms of solar cookers, solar heaters, photoelectric cells and solar canopies are not popular in hill areas. In the event of some technological breakthrough, the system of energy can certainly be introduced in those areas of the region where sunlight is abundantly available to save other degradable material resources. With the available present day technology, like solar energy, the prospects of exploiting wind energy are also not so bright, although the velocity of wind in hill areas, particularly at high altitudes, is very high.

**Conclusion**

Except a small proportion of commercial energy, that is used in long distance transportation, a few urban centres and very small number of industries, entire energy needs of the people of U.P. Himalayas is met by non-commercial energy resources. Energy is needed in household sector, which unlike in plains areas, is the largest energy consuming sector for cooking, space heating, lighting and water heating. Despite severe scarcity conditions, firewood occupies a predominant place as a free and reliable source of energy and expected to remain so in the long-run. Considering social, economic, climatic, geographical and environmental conditions of the region, a massive plantation drive should be launched. This will not only fulfil the firewood needs of the people but also restore the dying land, water, fodder, agriculture, flora, fauna and other material resources of the region to maintain a proper ecological balance which presently seems to be at stake. Any scheme of plantation and forestry could be made successful only when local people are taken into confidence to have their full cooperation and participation by ensuring their right over the planted trees and other forest resources.

The region presents a great potential of hydro-power as the beautiful system of small and big rivers, streams and narrow gorges flow full of water through out the area. This abundantly available renewable energy potential is yet to be harnessed for the well being of the society. Construction of big dams to exploit the power resource cannot be recommended in such an ecologically sensitive area where the costs incurred by these projects in terms of men material and overall environmental destruction are so high. To restore the ecological balance in the region and to bring an all-round development and welfare of it's people, the great hydro power prospects could be utilised as an alternative source of energy through mini and micro hydro projects with full cooperation and management of the local public. Electrification of the whole region with the power produced by these units will not only supplement the energy needs of the household sector but also bring greater diversification of economic activities in the hills.

Availability of sufficient organic waste materials for the use of bio-gas and bio-mass technology opens up great avenue for an another alternative source of energy in U.P. Himalayas. By over-coming numerous difficulties, as stated above, in the use of this organic waste material based system of energy, we would not only succeed in solving household energy problems of the people but also contribute in reducing the excessive burden on dwindling forest resources and thereby restore ecological stability in the region.

## REFERENCES

1. Shah, S.L. (1986): *Planning and Management of Natural and Human Resources in the Mountains*, Yatan Pubs., New Delhi.

2. Census of India (1991): Series-25, Paper-I of 1991, Uttar Pradesh.
3. *Ibid.*
4. SHERPA (1991): *Livestock Development in the Himalayan Regions of India : A Study*, Vol. I (Part-I & II), Lucknow.
5. Painuly, J.P.(1986): Household Energy Demand and Energy Supply Potential in Hill Areas, in Sherpa (ed.) Seminar Papers on Alternative Energy Systems for Hill Areas, Lucknow.
6. Kumar, Atul (1986): Utilisation of Non-Conventional Energy Sources in the Hill Region of the State of Uttar Pradesh in Sherpa (ed.) Seminar Papers on Alternative Energy Systems for Hill Areas, Lucknow.
7. Bahuguna, Sunder Lal (1993): Chhoti Panbijli Yojanaun Ki Prasangikata, *Nav-Bharat Times*, Lucknow, May 10.

TWELVE

# APPLICATION OF COMPUTERS FOR DEVELOPMENT PLANNING

ANJESH KUMAR

## Introduction

The use of computers is extending into a wide variety of applications ranging from maintenance of business books to computer-assisted surgery. A major area of development is in the use of computers by organisations to support management and decision-making. Some information systems are so large that researchers have proposed automation of many of the system-building functions.

Planning, organising and controlling are basic functions for decision-makers to give better performance. The key for the above functions is to get correct, accurate and timely information. For scientific analysis such as weather forecasting up-to-date classified information is needed. The earthquake victims could be saved by timely information and forecasting. It is better to distinguish between data, information and management information. 'Data' are raw, unanalysed facts from which information can be developed. 'Information' is analysed or processed data that informs the recipient about a situation. 'Management Information' is information that has action implications, that is, because it is accurate, timely and relevant because it represents all facets of a situation and decision-makers can determine from it what they must do about the situation.

For implementing, all this requires a systematic approach to manage the whole system. Management Information System (MIS) may be defined as a 'formal method of making available to management the accurate and timely information necessary to facilitate the decision-making process and enable the organisation's planning, control and operation function to be carried out effectively'. Here lies the role of Information Technology (IT). Today in every field of human activity IT has a very important role. It is a tool to help the decision-makers to arrive at a quick and better decision. Processing power does not substitute the human-end activity. One thing should be clear : IT is not a magic wand. That is a fact. Nor is it a panacea for all the troubles. IT is a method by which one speeds up the decision-making process, and does not reduce demands on human creativity and ingenuity. True, attempts are being made to replicate many parts of human thinking processes. But many of them directed at smoothing the man-machine interface, at making IT simpler and easier to handle.

The integration of these technologies is moving closer to the "paperless office" with electronic/computerised filing and retrieval, and a lot more. Voice and video interfaces to computers add new dimensions to the man-machine interface, with multi-media systems opening up, new avenues for computer applications. Management today has a wide range of options, and a fairly detailed understanding of technology is needed to make a wise choice. It is essential to plan out strategies for computerisation to handle changing environment and technology options.

In short, IT - from being a tool will get highly intertwined with our daily activities. The rules of human progress, business management and leadership will change. There's a lot we have to come to terms with (i) higher influence of information through IT on people will increase transparency of all activities, and (ii) for government and corporation access to information will no longer act as the differentiation; successful strategies will be increasingly dependence on the speed at which information is processed and how creatively analysis of such information one put to action.

The next century will herald the use of information and knowledge, when mankind will make the best use of IT to improve the efficicncy of socio-economic processes, and to enrich life.

Today, almost every area seems to have been covered by the computers. But, if go through those various developmental stages which the computers have been passing through we find that the scientists have really worked hard to put the computer in an accessible shape before the user.

During seventies the fourth generation computers have been developed with introducing Large Scale Integration (LSI), Very Large Scale Integration (VLSI) and Microprocessor – a 'chip' which by itself can perform the control, arithmetical and logical functions of a computer. The size was further reduced tremendously and an era for ushering more and more High Level Languages has set in. Simultaneously, readymade software/program is also being developed and a variety of computers are thus getting introduced. Networking has also been introduced in this generation of computers such that, one may have easy access to the information available at any other source, Railway Reservation is the most appropriate example of networking.

In the Fifth Generation computer (eighties onwards) Super Large Scale Integration (SLSI) and Very Large Scale Integrated Circuitry (VLSIC), speech synthesisers and artificial intelligence is being introduced.

Today we have the proud privelage of having very small and really handy – as small as the size of a brief-case, a note book or even a palm sized – computers. Such handy computers are in the real sense can be carried from place to place without any risk of their being damaged during the transit.

**Present Scenario**

Presently almost no area remains uncovered from the computers. Whether it is an area of medical science or weather forecasting; astrological predictions or music composing; fashion designing or share market; financial accounting or architecture or statistical analysis. The latest researches aimed at putting artificial intelligence into the computers with a view to ensuring that the suggestions/decisions or future planning is done through the computers. Earlier, most of the computers were capable of communicating in English only but with the outcome of the researches by the Indian scientists, today, one may use the computer in many of the Indian languages viz. Devnagari (Hindi), Tamil, Telgu, Kannada, Bangala, Oriya, Urdu etc. This, indeed, brings a revolution in India as far as the scope for the use of computers is concerned and today the computer users who do not know English can also have easy access to the computers and thus it puts the man and computer more proximate than they were in the past.

**Application of Computers in Research Areas**

Computers are also being used for research purposes in the fields of physical and social sciences where a lot of mathematics and statistical analysis is required to arrive at certain conclusions. Obviously, therefore, computer is the only operational and functional device to solve complex mathematics in a simple, accurate and fast manner. Social science researches are undertaken for the benefit of the society, therefore, the results ought to be precise and accurate so that the conclusions drawn and reports prepared on the basis of the results arrived at are such as would generally benefit the people of the society for whom the study was undertaken. This shows that the computers are necessary to get good and timely results.

Certain steps involved for the research purposes are as under :

(i) Selection of area or the universe of the study;
(ii) Formulation of a very precise research problem;
(iii) Formulation of schedules/questionnaire;
(iv) Collection of primary or the secondary data from the field;
(v) Analysis of primary and for secondary data;
(vi) Draw of the conclusions; and
(vii) Preparation of the report.

1. While making selection of the universe of the study we find that the computers are very useful and essential, tool for have the capacity of doing the same with accuracy and at a faster speed. For this we provide all information regarding the universe (area/region) on which basis the sample (individual area) is required to be selected, at times, randomly. For doing the random sampling we first decide the sample space and sample size then by the use of different softwares of programming techniques, sampling is done neatly and easily. Now, let us take an example. A study is required for the cause of low literacy level in 15 districts of three regions of Uttar Pradesh. Here, we need region-wise literacy rates for all the five regions of Uttar Pradesh. First we have to select three regions (sample size) from total of five regions (sample space) of UP, where the literacy rate is less as compared to other regions and then, the selection of five districts from each regions. Here, we require the literacy rate of all districts. The sample space may be all the districts of the region or it may be the number of districts where the literacy rate is less than the average rate of literacy for the entire region. This type of complex and random sample is very complicated if any one wishes to do it mannualy, but it is very easy for the computer to draw such type of samples. Feed all the informations regarding regions and districts

and instruct the conditions. The sample shall be ready within no time.

2. For preparation of the schedule we have to keep in mind the mode of analysis of the data, that is, whether the data are to be analysed on the computer or it have to be analysed manually. If it is to be analysed on computers then a lot of precautions have to be taken in advance.

3. For computer analysis we prepare our survey schedules in such a manner as the computer may be able to understand in terms of the definitions of the informations of schedules so canvassed. That is, we have to codify our probable answers of the questions in the schedule and preferably the questions should be of numeric nature, for calculations can be done on numerals only. Most important is to prepare questions single headed only. It is not such that each question is a combination of questions, for computer may analyse our data by combining different question. However, it is not possible to extract information from a question made of combinations of several questions.

4. After the preparation of survey schedules the primary data may be collected from the field by research investigators and the secondary data may also be collected from the census and other related handbooks. But, the collection of information from the previous studies is also a tedious job and it is quite difficult and in certain cases it is even impossible. Very often we do not get a bibliography or the studies, in full, from a single source (of the studies) for which the study is to be done. One library or publisher is not sufficient to yield all relevant information. But, by the use of latest technology on CD-ROM (Compact Disc Read Only Memory) it is very much possible to get information from a single source. CD-ROM is a plastic disc, of 4.72" in diametre, with a storage capacity of approximately 660 Megabyte which is roughly equal to 3,30,000 pages of text. Various types of CD-ROMs are available, some of them have bibliographies only, while some have the abstracts of the books also and few them have the full text. It is very fast in searching of information and the details may be had on monitor as well as on printer also. One more facility is available and that is ON-LINE retrieval system. It is a system which is linked with the national network and if you wish to have an information which is not available with your computer then you may get the required information from the other source by dialing

number provided the source along with us is linked with the network. One may have the information title-wise, author-wise or even publisher-wise. Since it is a new technology and it is not very popular for reasons of high cost of CD-ROM Drive and the subscriptions towards the CD-ROM discs.

Some of the CD-ROM Products are Shown in the Table

| S.No. | CD-ROM Product | Subjects Covered |
|---|---|---|
| 1. | Social Science Citation Index Compact Disc Editor (SSCI-CDE) | Social Science |
| 2. | Social Science Index | English literature, Anthropology, Economics |
| 3. | Applied Social Science Index and Abstracts (ASSIA) | Social Science |
| 4. | Sociofile | Social Science |
| 5. | PSYCLIT | Psychology (Journals) |
| 6. | AUSTROM | Education and Social Science |
| 7. | HELECON | Business, Management, Economics |
| 8. | Public Affair Information System (PAIS) | Social Science, Economics, Business and Finance, Political Science |
| 9. | POPOLINE (Population Studies) | Social Science, Statistics, Population and Demography |
| 10. | ERIC | Archives and Education |
| 11. | Books in Print Plus | All subjects |
| 12. | Ulrides Plus | Periodicals |
| 13. | LISA Plus | Library Information Science |

5. The most important part of the research is to analyse the primary and secondary data. This may also be done through the computer. For this one has to codify his/her data before feeding it into the computer. After feeding the data a number of statistical analysis are available may be done by using different statistical software packages. One may takeout the mean, median, mode, correlation, multiple regression etc. one may also test the hypothesis by applying different method of tests. Simultaneous equations for any number of unknowns variables may also be solved, matrix manipulations, cross tables etc. and above all one may also produce the graphs of different types viz. line, bar, stacked bar, pie etc. to support your analysis.

It is rarely necessary for an investigator to code a computer program to do statistical analysis because prewritten computer programs are available for almost all statistical analysis. The statistical programs are self contained set of programs which perform statistical analysis based on user specifications. The user must define the form of input data and specify the computation options desired.

A few of the most common general — purpose software packages are SPSS (Statistical Package for the Social Science) —A comprehensive program for processing common to the social sciences, BMDP and BMD (Biomedical Computer Programs), OMNITAB II – This is a large, unified set of computer routines to do statistical and numerical analysis.

Statistical Package for Social Sciences (SPSS) is the most popular software package used for statistical analysis in social science studies. The main analyses which may be obtained through this software are :

1. **Descriptive Statistics**
   a. *Frequencies*
      It gives frequency tables, statistics, bar charts and histograms.
   b. *Descriptives*
      It gives detailed statistics and optionally creates Z-Scores.
   c. *Cross Tables etc.*
      It gives bivariate distributions in the form of cross tabulation with measures of association.
   d. *Means*
      It gives means for sub-groups.
2. **Reports and Tables**
3. **Correlation and Regression**
   Correlation calculates the Pearson correlation coefficient for linear relationship and Regression estimates coefficients and significance tests for linear multiple regression models, and includes extensive residual analysis facilities. It also provides the facility to do Non-Linear Regression (NLR) analysis.
4. **Comparing Group Means**
   a. *T-Test*
      It tests for equality of means for both independent and paired samples.
   b. *Anova*
      It performs analysis of variance with multiple factors and covariates.
   c. *Oneway*

It performs analysis of variance with one factor, including multiple comparison tests.

d. *Manova*

It is a very powerful generalised analysis of variance and covariance.

5. **Classification and Clustering**
   a. Factor Analysis
   b. Cluster Analysis
   c. Descriminant Analysis

6. **Time Series**

   It is used for exponential-smoothing models, seasonal decomposition, Auto Correlation Function (ACF), partial auto correlation function, cross correlation function, Box-Jenkins analysis, evaluating the fit of a model and spectral analysis into cycles.

7. **Categories**
   a. Correspondence Analysis
   b. Homogeneity Analysis
   c. Conjoint Analysis etc.

8. **Other Analyses**
   a. Npar test
   b. Reliability
   c. Hiloglinear
   d. Loglinear

9. **Graph Data**

   It has the facility of plotting the scatterplots, control plots, overlay plots or contour plots and have the capability of producing graphs in the form of Pie charts, Bar charts, Line charts, Histograms etc.

6. The above discussion shows that by using the SPSS or other statistical softwares packages one may get all the analyses done and have very good results based on his/her data. Now, for getting the conclusions out of these results it is for us to draw inferences and finally have a very good and quality printed report for which we may use word-processing packages for printing our report. A number of wordprocessing packages are available e.g. WORDSTAR, MS-WORD, WORD PERFECT, VENTURA etc. By using these softwares we may have a very good and attractive report. But the main advantage of these software packages is to have the

facility of correcting the information very easily, one may remove words, lines, paragraphs or even pages as well as the facility of incorporating the new informations in between.

Hence, we may conclude that the role of computer in formulating a study is essentially very useful and it reflects that the results taken by the computer are much more accurate, and the most advantageous part is that it may be done very easily.

**Conclusion**

The government have been installing simultaneously providing computers to various offices and other important organisations with a view to rendering the services more efficiently and timely. After having installed the computer, any organisation/office requires computer personnel to handle it and make use of it. This manifests that the installation of computer creates new job opportunities and reduces the magnitude of unemployment which is, at present, one of the major problems the country is exposed to. To handle a computer is very easy provided one has a thorough training. The government have already encouraged the computer education, starting from the primary level of education to the university level. But, it is not mandatory for one to have his/her training from these institutions only, one may receive his/her training from any private institutions as well along with his/her present engagements. The government have also authorised certain private institutions to carry out their courses and make the person eligible for government jobs. This reflects that the government is trying to reduce the unemployment problem as well as introducing the latest technology to their offices to yield better results. But at the same time the fact which is gaining momentum among the people already working in the some organisation where the computers are just installed or are yet to be installed, feel that the computers are going to replace the man which is, however, not true. No machine can replace man because man is the only creature to have real intelligence. It is further also not necessary to be an engineer or a technical person for using the computer. One may use the computer very efficiently with his/her background in arts, commerce or science. All computers need is an aptitude for and knowledge of elementary mathematics.

Computer is doing the processing part only. For preparing a report on computer a lot of paper work is necessary, which is to be done manually, for the computer has just reduced the mechanical part of calculations. Therefore, one may utilise his/her time for the betterment of functioning rather than for simple additions and subtractions. Let us take the example of financial accounting. Before getting the cash book, ledger, trial balance, profit & loss account and balance sheet one has to prepare the vouchers, cheques and even checking or transferring of money from one account to another. Here, transfer of amounts may be done by the computer, but, one will have to decide which amount is to be transferred. For surveys, information from the field is to be collected by visiting the field and the reports are also to be drafted manually. This shows that before feeding the information into the computer a lot of work is to be done, and even after the generation of the report also. In most of the offices/organisations the personnel are being trained for using the computer and, ofcourse, some of the computer professionals are also appointed specifically for technical purposes. In some of the offices even typists are transferred to computer section for the purposes of data entry, for the keyboard of a computer is same as the keyboard of a manual English typewriter.

Hence, it may be worth reiterating that computer application/installation will not just result in raising the unemployment. In many of the private organisations employers are giving computer training to their non-technical staff with a view to increasing the efficiency and to reducing the mechanical (and the duplication of) work. Now, the strength of the staff is being utilised for a better structured and systematic functioning and also for improving the overall system.

## REFERENCES

Davis, Gordan B. : *Introduction to Computers*, McGraw-Hill, Kogakusha Ltd.

D'Souza, Eric S. : *Chippin In* : SKW Enterprises, New Delhi.

Stoner, James A.F. : *Management*, Prentice-Hall of India Pvt. Ltd., New Delhi.

Subramanian, L. : 'Managing through Technology', *PC Quest*, Vol. 5, No. 10, October 1993.

Subramanian, N. : *Computers — Genesis, Programming and Applications*, A.H. Wheeler & Co. Pvt. Ltd., Allahabad.

Subramanian, N and Kannan, N. : *Exploring Your PC with BASIC*, A.H. Wheeler & Co., Pvt. Ltd., Allahabad.

# INDEX